30p

NGLISH LANGUAGE AND LITERATURE

for AQA

Alison Ross

Heinemann

Published by Heinemann Educational Publishers, Halley Court, Jordan Hill, Oxford OX2 8EJ
A division of Reed Educational and Professional Publishing Ltd

OXFORD MELBOURNE AUCKLAND
JOHANNESBURG BLANTYRE GABORONE
IBADAN PORTSMOUTH (NH) USA CHICAGO

First published 2001

05 04 03 02 01
10 9 8 7 6 5 4 3 2 1

0 435 10978 2

ACKNOWLEDGEMENTS

The publishers gratefully acknowledge the following for permission to reproduce copyright material. Every effort has been made to trace copyright holders, but in some cases has proved impossible. The publishers would be happy to hear from any copyright holder that has not been acknowledged.

Extract from *A Plot of My Own* in *TES* 4th July 1997. © Times Supplements Ltd, 1997; used with permission. Extract from *Talking Heads II* by Alan Bennett. Copyright © Alan Bennett; reprinted by permission of Peters Fraser & Dunlop on behalf of Alan Bennett. Extract from *Art* by Yasmina Retz, translated by Christopher Hampton, published by Faber & Faber Ltd; reprinted by permission of the publishers. Extract from *A Farewell To Arms* by Ernest Hemingway, published by Jonathan Cape; used by permission of The Random House Group Ltd. Extract from *Shooting an Elephant* by George Orwell. Copyright © George Orwell 1936; reproduced by permission of A.M. Heath & Co. Ltd, on behalf of Bill Hamilton as the Literary Executor of the Estate of the Late Sonia Brownell and Martin Secker & Warburg Ltd. Extract from editorial in *Bliss* reproduced with the kind permission of Emap Elan Syndication. Extract from *Glamorama* by Bret Easton Ellis, published by Picador 1999. Copyright © Bret Easton Ellis 1998; reproduced by permission of the author c/o Rogers, Coleridge & White Ltd, 20 Powis Mews, London W11 1JN in association with International Creative Managements, New York. Extract from *The Kenneth Williams Diaries*; reprinted by permission of Peters Fraser & Dunlop Ltd on behalf of the Estate of Kenneth Williams. Extract from a letter by Count Nikolai Tolstoy which appeared in the *Daily Telegraph*, 2nd August 2000. Copyright © Nikolai Tolstoy; reproduced by permission of A.M. Heath & Co. Ltd. Extract from *Lifting The Latch* by Sheila Stewart, published by Oxford University Press 1987. Copyright © Sheila Stewart; reprinted by permission of Oxford University Press. Extract from *The BFG* by Roald Dahl, published by Jonathan Cape and Penguin Books; reprinted by permission of David Higham Associates Ltd. Extract from the Sports pages of the *Guardian*, 2nd October 2000. Copyright © the *Guardian*; used with permission. Extract from *Playstation Zone*, April 1998; reprinted with permission of the old editors of *Playstation Zone*, which is no longer in print. Extracts from *Brave New World* by Aldous Huxley, published by Flamingo 1994. Copyright © Aldous Huxley; reprinted with the kind permission of the author's agent, The Reece Halsey Agency, USA. Extract from *The Loneliness of the Long Distance Runner* by Alan Sillitoe. Copyright © Alan Sillitoe 1959, 1987; reprinted by permission of Rosica Colin Ltd. Extract from *The New Dress* by Virginia Woolf; reprinted by permission of The Society of Authors as the Literary Representative of the Estate of Virginia Woolf. Extract from *Small Avalanches* by Joyce Carol Oates; reprinted with the kind permission of the author. Extract from *The Vet's Daughter* by Barbara Comyns; reprinted by permission of John Johnson (Authors' Agent) Ltd. Extract from *Rope* by Katherine Anne Porter, from *Collected Stories of Katherine Anne Porter* by Katherine Anne Porter, published by Jonathan Cape; used by permission of The Random House Group Ltd. Extract from *The Secret Diary of Adrian Mole* by Sue Townsend; used by permission of The Random House Group Ltd. Extract from *Writing Skills* by Tricia Hedge, published by Longman. Extract from *Way Home* by Libby Hathorn, published by Andersen Press Ltd; reprinted with permission of the publishers. Extract from *The Bitch Rules* by Elizabeth Wurtzel, published by Quartet Books Ltd; used with permission. Extract from *Happy Endings (Murder in the dark: Short fictions and prose poems)* by Margaret Atwood. Copyright © Margaret Atwood 1983; reproduced with permission of Curtis Brown Ltd on behalf of Margaret Atwood. Extract from *Tulip Fever* by Deborah Moggach, published by Heinemann; used by permission of The Random House Group Ltd. Extract from *Silent Playgrounds* by Danuta Reah, published by HarperCollins 2000; reprinted by permission of the publishers. Extract from *On dumbing down for men* by Shane Watson, in the *Guardian* 24th March 2000. Copyright © Shane Watson, 24th March, 2000; used with permission. Extract from *If you're busy busy busy, you're really thick thick thick* by Julie Burchill, in the *Guardian Weekend Magazine*; reprinted by permission of Capel & Land on behalf of Julie Burchill.

Typeset by TechType, Abingdon, Oxon
Printed and bound by Bath Press in the UK

Contents

This book offers a structured approach to the study of the new AS English Language and Literature courses available from September 2000.

Like all AS courses, the English Language and Literature course consists of three modules. You may work through each of the modules in turn in your course, taking the first exam in January, or your teachers may decide to present elements of all three throughout the year and enter you for the June exams. Whichever course you plan to follow, it is best to start working through Module 1, 'Introduction to Language and Literature Study', as it provides the basic concepts and terms that are developed in Modules 2 and 3.

Literary and linguistic terminology and the glossaries

As you work through the book you will be introduced to important literary and linguistic terms. Words in **bold text** are explained in the glossary at the end of the book. It is advisable to keep a personal glossary of terms with your own explanations and examples. These will serve as a useful revision source and allow you to check your own learning progress.

Assessment Objectives

It is important to know exactly what you are being tested on. Sometimes in education, it is not clear and everyone is too polite to ask. For example, students are often told that their essays are 'too subjective', but what exactly do the terms 'subjective' and 'objective' mean?

The situation is different in other areas of life. Suppose you entered a driving test with your own notion of what constitutes good driving. You might model yourself on a racing driver and try to go as fast as possible without hitting anything. You might attempt to be stylish and drive with one hand on the wheel and the other leaning on the window as you chatted to the examiner. Instead you approach the test knowing that it requires specific skills. The test booklet lists these clearly and the examiner checks whether you satisfy each one. You know, for example, that you must be able to reverse round a corner, do a three-point turn and an emergency stop. For each of these skills, there are further requirements that differentiate a pass from a fail. Sometimes these requirements are not obvious from the initial description. A three-point turn does not have to be executed in three moves. You can make five, or even more, moves and still pass this skill. But you will fail if you touch the kerb at any point. Knowing this gives every learner driver a fair opportunity to practise and achieve the manoeuvre.

In order to have this 'fair opportunity' when you study for AS and A2 Level exams, you need to understand the Assessment Objectives. The wording alone may not be enough. Like the term 'three-point turn', Objectives may need further explanation to make the requirements absolutely clear. The aim of this introductory section is to make clear what skills and knowledge the exam is testing. It also aims to explain the different levels of achievement, i.e. what is needed to achieve higher grades as opposed to a pass. There will be further explanations and examples, as you work through the material in the book. First, some clarification of the words used in the Assessment Objectives:

AS and A Level study require a combination of *knowledge*, *understanding* and *skills*. These three are closely linked and overlap, but there is a distinction. To take the analogy of cookery:

Knowledge of facts: Ingredients
Quantities
Heat
Time

Understanding: Food types (so that you can substitute honey for sugar)
How temperature affects different foods (you don't need to know 'why' as a domestic cook)

Skills: Manual – chopping, whisking, etc.
Organisational – sequence and timing
Visual – presentation

Of course, this may seem unnecessarily complicated. For most of us, the only test of our cookery is whether people enjoyed eating the meal, perhaps whether it was also cheap and nutritious and didn't give anyone food poisoning. We don't learn to cook by differentiating objectives. But if there was a cookery test, it would be useful to know exactly what was required.

AS Objectives

There are six Assessment Objectives for the study of Language and Literature. The only difference between AS and A Level is in the depth and breadth of the requirements. These are the Objectives for AS Level:

1 Communicate clearly the knowledge, understanding and insights gained from the combination of literary and linguistic study, using appropriate terminology and accurate written expression.

2 In responding to literary and non-literary texts, distinguish, describe and interpret variation in meaning and form.

3 Respond to and analyse texts, using literary and linguistic concepts and approaches.

4 Show understanding of the way contextual variation and choices of form, style and vocabulary shape the meaning of texts.

5 Identify and consider the ways attitudes and values are created and conveyed in speech and writing.

6 Demonstrate expertise and accuracy in writing for a variety of specific purposes and audiences, drawing on knowledge of literary texts and features of language to explain and comment on the choices made.

First consider what *skills* are needed – in other words, what you must be able to do. You may not be confident yet about identifying verbs, but one way is to see if the word will fit into a phrase like 'I must be able to _____ '. Some of the skills are straightforward and others are more complex.

You must be able to:

- **identify**
- **describe**
- **draw** on knowledge of literary texts and features of language
- **use** appropriate terminology and accurate written expression
- **distinguish**
- **demonstrate** expertise and accuracy
- **communicate** clearly
- **write** for a variety of purposes and audiences
- **explain**
- **consider**
- **comment**
- **analyse**
- **show** understanding
- **respond**
- **interpret**.

The activities in the modules explain what is involved in the skills of analysing, responding and interpreting, as these are essential for higher grades.

Now consider what you need to know and understand. The nouns in the Assessment Objectives list these aspects. If you are not confident yet about identifying nouns, a good test is to see whether the word fits into a phrase like 'I need to know/understand _____ '. It makes little sense to say that you *know* something without understanding it, but there are areas of new material that you will have to become familiar with. These are listed first. Other areas do not rely so much on acquiring new knowledge, as on developing your understanding. These come later in the list.

You need to know / understand:

- **texts** (literary and non-literary)

- **terminology** (literary and linguistic)
- **features** of language
- **variation** in context, meaning, form, style, vocabulary
- **choices** in meaning, form, style, vocabulary
- **concepts** literary and linguistic
- **approaches** literary and linguistic
- **attitudes** and the way they are created in speech and writing
- **values** and the way they are created in speech and writing
- **meanings** of texts.

Rather than offering a brief, abstract definition of these terms and concepts now, the book contains activities that will gradually make each term or concept clearer. As you develop the necessary knowledge, understanding and skills, the meaning of the concepts should emerge. Important concepts and terminology will be printed in bold when an activity focuses on them.

Asking questions

Each module in this book contains:

- *teaching text* that introduces concepts with examples and explanations of important terms
- *activities* that set tasks and ask questions, often based on extracts
- *commentaries* that provide suggested responses based on the author's interpretation.

Be prepared, as you study English Language and Literature, to challenge these interpretations and offer alternative viewpoints. It takes confidence to do this, but a good way to start is by asking honest questions. This is not as easy as it sounds. A Philosophy tutor helpfully told his students at the beginning of the lesson: 'If there is any word you don't understand, just ask.' None of the students spoke for the remainder of the session. One student later explained the problem: 'I understood each individual word, but I didn't understand what you meant.'

In this AS course, for example, the phrase 'contextual variation' occurs in one Assessment Objective. Suppose that you ask what this means and are given the explanation: 'It means variation in context.' This doesn't actually help, as you still need to know what the term 'context' refers to in language and literature. One question and one explanation are rarely enough when people are learning something, particularly if it is complex and abstract – it usually takes several attempts from the learner and teacher.

Key Skills

This AS course in English Language and Literature provides opportunities to produce evidence in aspects of Key Skills. Activities are marked with a Key Skills symbol where relevant, e.g. **IT3.1A**

Communication	
C3.1a	Contribute to discussions
C3.1b	Make a presentation
C3.2	Read and synthesise information
C3.3	Write different types of documents
Information technology	
IT3.1	Plan and select information
IT3.2	Develop information
IT3.3	Present information
Working with others	
WO3.1	Plan the activity
WO3.2	Work towards agreed objectives
WO3.3	Review the activity
Improving own learning and performance	
LP3.1	Agree and plan targets
LP3.2	Seek feedback and support
LP3.3	Review progress
Problem solving	
PS3.1	Recognise, explain and describe the problem
PS3.2	Generate and compare different ways of solving problems
PS3.3	Plan and implement options
PS3.4	Agree and review approaches to tackling problems

Definitions of Key Skills indicated

MODULE (1) Introduction to Language and Literature Study

This module counts for 35% of the AS qualification, or 17.5% of the total A Level marks.

ASSESSMENT OBJECTIVES

The skills and knowledge that you develop in this module, and that will be assessed in your coursework, are defined by the examination board's Assessment Objectives. These require that you:

1 communicate clearly the knowledge, understanding and insights gained from the combination of literary and linguistic study, using appropriate terminology and accurate written expression
   (5% of the final AS mark; 2.5% of the final A Level mark)

2 distinguish, describe and interpret variation in meaning and form in responding to literary and non-literary texts
   (10% of the final AS mark; 5% of the final A Level mark)

3 respond to and analyse texts, using literary and linguistic concepts and approaches
   (10% of the final AS mark; 5% of the final A Level mark)

4 show understanding of the ways contextual variation and choices of form, style and vocabulary shape the meanings of texts
   (5% of the final AS mark; 2.5% of the final A Level mark)

5 identify and consider the ways attitudes and values are created and conveyed in speech and writing
   (5% of the final AS mark; 2.5% of the final A Level mark).

The focus of this module is an anthology of literary and non-literary texts on a common theme. The exam will test both your knowledge and understanding of the texts in this anthology and the skills you have developed in 'critical assessment'. This means reading with awareness of the ways in which texts work. The first question deals with the central collection of poetry; the second question focuses on the remaining texts in the anthology.

So there are two important strands to your study:

1 The most obvious is the set text – the anthology.

2 It is equally important to understand and apply the literary and linguistic concepts and approaches. Some will be familiar from GCSE study, in particular literary concepts such as 'metaphor', which will be explored in more detail. The linguistic concepts may be less familiar, so this module provides a clear framework for describing language and shows how these concepts can be applied to your study of texts.

A systematic framework for language analysis

What is language? One definition states that it is 'a structured system for communicating meanings'.

The following table represents the structure of language as a hierarchy – building up from the smallest units to the largest. Although there is a glossary at the end of the book, you should create your own collection of terms and examples. This framework provides a way of organising your notes.

Discourse *text type and structure*	**Semantics** *meanings*	**Pragmatics** *implied meanings*
Phonology *sounds* **Graphology** *marks* on the page/screen	**Morphology** word *structure* **Lexis** *words*	**Grammar** *sentence structure*

The structure of language as a hierarchy

Here is a brief explanation of the terms, but you will find more detail and examples of each as you work through the module.

Discourse refers to the study of how language works beyond the level of the single sentence. It involves study of the way particular **genres** (types) of texts are structured. A telephone conversation and a business letter begin and end in different ways, for example. It also involves study of the text's **context**, including whether it was written or spoken, its purpose and audience. But once you start to analyse how these longer texts work, you usually need to refer back to smaller units, such as individual words, or even sounds.

Semantics is the study of how meanings are constructed, not just the dictionary definition that could be fed into a computer, but all the associated meanings. Could a computer discern the difference in meaning between the following terms, which are apparently similar in meaning?

'I am strong-minded.' / 'You are obstinate.' / 'He is a pig-headed fool.'

As an experienced user of the language you are sensitive to such shades of meaning, but may need to learn technical terms such as **connotation** to refer to the negative or positive impact of words.

Pragmatics is the study of language in use. This involves the fascinating way that meanings are often implied and cannot be understood simply by knowledge of the sounds, words and grammar of a language. For example, the following utterance from a parent to a child.

'That's right. Leave all your clothes all over the floor.'

Analysis of the sentence structure of this utterance would show that it is a congratulation, followed by an instruction. Every child understands its meaning to be quite different.

Phonology deals with the smallest units of language. These are the sounds in the case of spoken language.

Graphology is the study of visual signs – the marks on the page or screen in written language. The way a text looks – the size or type of font, for example, can affect the meaning.

Sounds or marks are combined to form words, but there is a smaller unit in between:

Morphology looks at the way that words are formed from smaller units of meaning – *morphemes*. The word, un-reli-able, for example, is formed from three morphemes. The **prefix** (un-) adds a negative sense to the **base** (rely) and the **suffix** (-able) includes the concept of ability.

Lexis refers to the individual words used. You may be more familiar with the term 'vocabulary' or the term 'diction' when discussing the type of words used in literary texts. It does not matter which term you use.

Grammar refers to structure, i.e. how words are combined to form meanings. The study of sentence grammar used to be the main concern of English lessons, in the era when children had to pass an 11+ exam to go to a grammar school. Since then, the study of language has gone much further than analysis of **sentence structure,** and looks at text grammar and speech grammar. However, the term 'grammar' is used by most people to refer to the structure of **sentences**. This area of grammar can seem daunting for various reasons. Millions of words have been written analysing the sentence structure of English. Don't worry – you only need a basic toolkit of concepts and terms to analyse sentence grammar. Remember that the sentence is only one of the interesting levels of language. It is rare to encounter language as single sentences, except in textbook exercises. You usually encounter longer stretches of language in, for example, conversations, adverts, articles, TV programmes, books.

These examples should demonstrate that a study of grammar is just one aspect of an understanding of the meanings that language communicates. In your study of texts, it is essential to begin at the highest points of the hierarchy, i.e. the discourse, semantics and pragmatics. This is also the best point for users of the language with more than sixteen years' experience of operating this system, generally understanding what is meant and implied, without having analysed the smaller units that contribute to that meaning. It is then fascinating to dig deeper and analyse – *how* were these meanings constructed? To do this, you will need to refer to the word choice, or the sentence structure, or even smaller units such as sounds, visual signs and morphemes.

You should follow this approach in your study and in the exam:

- begin with the 'large' issues of genre, audience, purpose and context
- then move to the smaller details of language.

If you only make general observations about the text, your points will seem too *subjective*. This means that you have stated your opinion, but, because you have not provided any supporting evidence, another person could just as easily offer a different view. If, on the other hand, you simply describe some features of vocabulary and grammar, the points lack significance, even if these seem like *objective* facts. Comments like, 'There are five adjectives and the sentences are complex' invite the response, 'So what?' Activity 1 shows how you can bridge the gap between your observations about the context and meaning of the text and some objective points about the way the language is structured.

ACTIVITY 1

Read the following text, which was seen on the back of a bus, and discuss the following questions in small groups.

1 What type of text is it?   DISCOURSE – genre
2 What is its purpose?   DISCOURSE – purpose
3 Is the situation of the reader important?   DISCOURSE – audience
4 What are the implied meanings?   PRAGMATICS
5 Does the form of the text resemble another genre?   DISCOURSE – genre
6 What do you notice about the sentence structure?   GRAMMAR
7 What do you notice about the choice of words?   LEXIS and SEMANTICS
8 What do you notice about the visuals?   GRAPHOLOGY

Now read the commentary on page 43.

You'll never sleep.
She'll never wake.

Don't drink and drive.

Ways of reading an anthology

Let's return to the task of studying the set text, but use the concepts outlined above to find useful ways of reading an anthology. You can make *brief* marginal notes on the text and take it into the exam room. More detailed comments should be kept separately in a folder.

It is useful to understand what an anthology is, as this will influence the way that you read it. The word 'anthology' comes from Greek: 'anthos' means flower and '-logia' means gathering, so the literal meaning is 'a gathering of flowers'. The term is now used to refer to a 'choice gathering of writings'. Think about how the choice was made – what do the texts share in common and how do they differ? Some anthologies are collections of the writings of a particular author; the anthologies used in this syllabus are a more diverse collection of texts with a common theme or topic. The texts are diverse in various ways: different writers, genres, historical and social contexts, for example.

You do not have to read an anthology from cover to cover, starting at page 1, as you would with a novel. The texts may have been grouped in helpful ways by the person who compiled the anthology, but it is possible to choose your own route through the texts, finding your own connections.

The following activities look at ways of grouping the texts according to:

- genre – literary v. non-literary
    - text types
    - **speech** v. **writing**
- perspective – 1st v. 3rd person
- purpose and audience
- historical and social context
- attitudes and values.

Before an *intensive* reading of each text, you should start by using other reading techniques. *Skimming* refers to a quick reading for gist. *Scanning* is reading to find a particular piece of information (for example, the way you would read a train timetable to see if there was a train to Birmingham in the early morning and, if so, which platform it leaves from). The following activities require you to make an initial reading of the anthology, using skimming and scanning to get an overview of the diversity of the texts and begin to make connections between them.

Literary and non-literary texts

The first distinction is at the level of discourse. What genre (type of text) is each one? The syllabus states that there is a mixture of *literary* and non-literary texts, but what exactly is the difference? This question is not as simple as it may sound. Everyone is used to studying 'English' up to GCSE, often with no distinction made between Literature lessons and Language lessons. At AS and A Level, the names of the exams suggest there is a difference: there is a choice between studying English Literature, English Language or – in your case – English Language and Literature. One of the aims of this course is to 'encourage students to study language and literature as interconnecting disciplines'. But before you look at the connections between language and literature, it's worth exploring the differences.

ACTIVITY 2   C3.1A

1   Write down your own definition of each term: language and literature.

2   Now try a 'pyramiding' exercise. The ideal number of students for this is sixteen, but the principle is that you gradually increase the size of the discussion group until the whole class is working together.

   • Work in pairs first. Compare definitions with a partner and find the similar ideas. You may not have used exactly the same words.

   • Join up with another pair and see whether the four of you share any ideas.

   • Repeat this once or twice until the whole group is involved. See if there is any general consensus about the definitions of language and literature. Do 'great minds think alike'? Or are there some interesting disagreements?

3   Compare your definitions with those in a dictionary. If there are a number of definitions given, concentrate on the *first* one. The number [1] indicates that the definition following is the most common, or the most significant sense of the word. What are the key words in each definition, i.e. the ideas that most people in your class mentioned?

Now read the commentary on pages 43–44.

ACTIVITY 3

For this activity, you should play 'devil's advocate' – someone who states the case against a proposal for the sake of argument. Challenge the definition of literature (given in the commentary for Activity 2) by giving examples of:

- texts that you value and enjoy, but that may not be generally accepted as literature.

Try to give examples of:

- written texts whose language is *not* beautiful, but which have an emotional effect
- beautifully written texts that do *not* have an emotional effect
- texts that have an emotional effect and beautiful language, but are *listened* to rather than read from a page.

Compare your examples in groups of three or four and report back to the full group.

Now read the commentary on pages 44–45.

Genre

The term 'genre' refers to the form, or type, of text. Here is a brief definition: A genre is a set of conventions that govern the way particular texts are written for particular purposes. The genre of essay, for example, conventionally uses an impersonal style to put forward a clear argument, beginning with an introduction and ending with a concluding paragraph. The writer of the text works within these conventions and the reader approaches the text with similar expectations. This explains comments written in the margin by teachers like, 'Where is your introduction?', 'Don't use slang', 'Too much personal opinion'.

Of course, these conventions may vary from one cultural context to another and gradually change over time. The author's contact with students of English as an alternative language has provided many fascinating insights into the way language works. One Japanese student of Business English produced a letter to the bank manager beginning with the observation, 'Spring is approaching and the almond trees are in blossom.' It was sad to explain to her that it is not conventional in our culture to begin business letters with a general comment about the season. Perhaps this will change – certainly there is a gradual move towards the personal in business correspondence.

Sometimes there is a deliberate mixture of genres. Advertisements often disguise themselves as other texts. Junk mail attempts to look like a personal letter, often using a typeface that resembles handwriting, but the opening 'Dear Occupier' is a give-away. There are apparent articles in newspapers whose only clue to their true identity is the words 'advertising feature' in small print at the top.

It is important to know what genre of text you are reading, so that you appreciate the normal conventions and do not expect it to fulfil some other requirements. If you are reading the transcript of a conversation, you can expect to find hesitations and repetitions; an account of a true story may not have an 'ending' in the same way as a fictional narrative; a magazine article is likely to plunge in without an introduction. It is not helpful to identify points in a negative way and complain that a text lacks the features of a different genre, for example, 'This conversation is very disjointed and has no clear ending.'

The traditional use of the term 'genre' is to distinguish types of literature: poetry, prose and drama. Each can then be sub-divided. Prose can take the form of novels, short stories, autobiography, travel writing, etc. Novels can be sub-divided into genres such as romance, thriller, sci-fi, horror.

The term 'genre' is used now to classify other types of language, including spoken forms, such as lectures, interviews, speeches, conversations, TV documentaries, sermons. The context clearly influences the form and style. Apart from the factors of purpose and audience, it makes a difference whether the language is spontaneous or scripted; whether there is a single speaker or interaction between several. Remember that poetry and drama are *essentially* spoken forms. Their primary audience is a listening audience, though the study of poetry and drama in education means that the primary purpose is often forgotten and the poems and plays are studied on the page.

ACTIVITY 4   C3.2

Skim and scan read the anthology in order to categorise the texts.

- Decide whether each is a literary or non-literary text. There may be cases where you cannot decide. Note this as an interesting discussion point.

- Identify the genre of each.

- List the genres and group them to show connections.

Now read the commentary on page 45, which refers to the anthology.

Speech and writing

It is important to be aware of the different modes, or channels, for language. We can communicate via sounds, visual marks on the page or gestures. We use language in different ways depending on whether we are speaking or writing, so this is a significant aspect of the context. All the texts in the anthology are examples of writing in the sense that they are represented by marks on the page, rather than by sounds. However, some of the texts are written versions of spoken language, intended to be listened to rather than read. This means that a reader cannot judge the full effect, unless it is read aloud.

Type of writing	Example
Originally spoken language – spontaneous, but recorded and transcribed later	A conversation or live interview
Originally written language – scripted to be read aloud and listened to	A documentary programme, a play, or some poems and stories
A written text, which represents speech, but is intended to be read silently	Novels, poems and articles that include monologue or dialogue
A written text without any representation of speech	An instruction manual, a business letter, some poems and articles

ACTIVITY 5

C3.2

Scan the texts in the anthology and group them, using the four categories suggested above.

No commentary.

You may be working on your coursework folder as you study for this module. It is a requirement in Module 3 that you produce one text for a listening audience, so you will have the chance to construct a text that is intended to be spoken aloud. (In Module 4 you may decide to adapt a written text into a spoken form, such as a play script.)

Activity 11 in Module 3 (page 140) will give you some experience of transforming spoken language into a written representation. This should make you more aware of the different ways that language is crafted to appeal to listeners or readers. The insights you gain should also inform your understanding and analysis of the texts in the anthology that include representation of speech.

Reading transcripts

Because a **transcript** looks so different from conventional written language, it can be difficult to read from the page. A transcript of speech represents the words spoken as accurately as possible, but does not use the punctuation conventions of written language such as full stops and commas. **Pauses** may be shown with a row of dots. Some transcripts try to show emphasis with capital letters, bold or italic text, but spelling conventions are not changed to represent the pronunciation. As the listener cannot be sure where a sentence begins and ends, capital letters are only used for **proper nouns** (see page 22).

A transcript looks disjointed and muddled, but this doesn't mean that spoken language is not as clear as written language. It simply works in different ways. Activity 6 explores some of the ways in which spoken language works.

ACTIVITY 6

Listen to someone reading a transcript aloud. Then look at the printed version.

- Did you find the spoken version easier to follow than the written?

- What parts of the transcript made it difficult to read?

Now read the commentary on pages 45–46.

EXTRACT (ANTHOLOGY: FROM TEXT 2 *THE NAVAL SISTER'S TALE*)

(A nurse is talking about her experiences working on a hospital ship during the Second World War.)

NAVAL SISTER: Yes ... however ... every two hours we had to go round and because of this awful pitch and to ... roll ... I was seasick ... and ... hoped ... it was the most ghastly this to be at this ... for three nights I was seasick ... but still carried ... had managed to get round ... and normally one would do one's round in perhaps an hour all being well with injections ... but it would take me my two hours ... by the time I got back to my ... office where the ... the ... the Chinese steward would be bringing me my cup of tea and sandwiches to keep me going during the nights ... sort of thing ... it was time for me to start again ... I could never get a sit down because of this ... and ... the other sis ... the other sister too ... we were both green with ... green with seasickness and ... however ... after three days we were miraculously cured and yet we were still pitching and tossing and rolling ...

INTERRUPTION 6: Yes ... but could you stand it ... isn't it queer?

NAVAL SISTER: It is ... yes ... we were ... we ... we seemed to be cured and up till that time I thought ... I shall have to resign from the navy ... say I can't do any more ... get me flown home or something ... I could not do it and had we been torpedoed I very definitely would have gone for the boats ... I would like ... death was preferable at that time ... and ... I came ... this ... it's the most worst kind ... ever had a feeling like that in my life before or since ...

Written representations of speech

The purpose of a transcript is to provide an accurate word-for-word version of the words spoken. Other written texts represent speech in ways that capture the 'flavour' of the spoken voice, but make it easier for the reader and / or the listener. The genre of dramatic **monologue**, for example, has been used by Alan Bennett to create a strong sense of an individual's speaking voice, but the written version differs from spontaneous speech.

ACTIVITY 7

Read the extract from *Talking Heads II: Miss Fozzard Finds her Feet*, by Alan Bennett.

- What impression does this extract give of the character?
- Identify features of spoken language – both vocabulary and sentence structure.
- What features of spontaneous spoken language are missing?

Now read the commentary on page 46.

> Bit of a bombshell today. I'm just pegging up me stocking when Mr Sudaby says: 'I'm afraid, Miss Fozzard, this is going to be our last encounter.' Apparently, this latest burglary's put the tin hat on things, and what with Mrs Sudaby's mother finally going into a home, and their TV reception always being so bad, there's not much to keep them in Leeds so they're making a bolt for it and heading off to Scarborough. Added to which, Tina, their chow, has a touch of arthritis so the sands may help, and the upshot is they've gone in for a little semi near Peasholme Park.

ACTIVITY 8   C3.3   LP3.2

- Produce a written version of the transcript you studied in Activity 6.
- Read another person's version and comment on the changes made.
- What impression do you get of the speaker's personality and feelings?

Now read the commentary on page 47.

Structure of oral narratives

Although oral (spoken) narratives may be relatively spontaneous, they are still structured, even if the planning happens subconsciously. From studying many recordings of people telling stories, the American researcher William Labov has identified a six-part structure in oral narratives. Some of these features can be seen in the student's planned retelling of the story given in the commentary to Activity 8, although the student was not aware of **Labov's framework**. Are they present in your version?

- *Abstract*: What, in brief, is the story about? (I wouldn't wish seasickness on anyone)
- *Orientation*: Who, when, where, what? (rounds on the ship, ... me and the other sister)

- *Complicating action*: Then what happened? (ghastly pitch and roll)

- *Evaluation*: So, how is this interesting? (green with seasickness all night)

- *Result or resolution*: What finally happened? (after three days the sickness stopped)

- *Coda*: That's it; my story has ended and I'm bringing you back to the present situation. (Death or seasickness, I know what I'd choose!)

Oral narratives are usually told in the **1st person** – factual accounts about what 'I' did. Written narratives can be written in either 1st or **3rd person** – referring to all the characters as 'he' or 'she'. The variation in **perspective** is explored further in Module 2, page 88. For now, simply identify the perspective and leave comment and analysis till a later stage.

ACTIVITY 9	**C3.2**

Scan the texts in the anthology.

- Which are written from a 1st-person perspective?

As well as factual accounts, there may be some prose fiction and poetry that is written from the perspective of an individual.

No commentary.

Telling a story in 3rd-person narrative

The narrator of a story about another person can make an observer's comments about the person's actions and feelings. Perhaps the person involved would not have been able to make those comments. The events and feelings may be described in a precise and careful vocabulary, that would not have occurred to the person involved.

These features are apparent in the following extract from *The Red Badge of Courage*, by Steven Crane (Text 13 in the War anthology). The feelings of a young soldier are described in a thoughtful manner, though the individual caught up in the situation would be unlikely to come up with such calm, analytical reflections. The vocabulary used by the narrator is more **formal** and complex than a speaker would use, particularly this young character.

This advance of the enemy had seemed to the youth like a ruthless hunting. He began to fume with rage and exasperation. He beat his foot upon the ground, and scowled with hate at the swirling smoke that was approaching like a phantom flood. There was a maddening quality in this seeming resolution of the foe to give him no rest, to give him no time to sit down and think. Yesterday he had fought and had fled rapidly. There had been many adventures. For today he felt that he had earned opportunities for contemplative repose.

ACTIVITY 10   WO3.1   WO3.2   WO3.3

You will need a tape recorder for this activity. You may find it helpful to warm up first by talking in small groups about a recent event or experience that was memorable in some way – it was funny, exciting or embarrassing, for example.

- Record your brief anecdote about this occasion.

- Transcribe the tape using the conventions outlined on page 9.

- Take another person's transcript and re-write it as a 3rd-person account, making any changes necessary to create a readable narrative.

- Note the changes made to your own anecdote as a 3rd-person account.

- List the texts in the anthology that are written from a 3rd-person perspective.

Now read the commentary on page 47.

Written representations of dialogue

A number of texts in the anthology represent conversations. The term **dialogue** refers to spoken interaction involving more than one person, whereas 'monologue' refers to the speech of a single person. There are various ways of representing spoken dialogue in written texts. The graphology differs in the type of punctuation and line spacing used. There are also different choices of vocabulary and sentence structure.

Drama is represented on the page as a play script, which simply writes the speaker's name followed by the words spoken. Stage directions are added in a different type style – italics or capital letters. Apart from occasional directions, the tone of voice is left to the actor's interpretation. Drama scripts represent conversation and interaction between people in a way that may seem close to natural speech, but the speech is crafted for dramatic purposes – to indicate the underlying relationships between characters, for example.

ACTIVITY 11   C3.2

Two people should read the dialogue from *Art*, by Yasmina Retz (translated by Christopher Hampton) aloud.

- What impression does this conversation give about the two characters and their friendship?

- In what ways is the script like a natural conversation?

- The characters say little out loud. What do you, as the audience, imagine that each is thinking but not saying?

- What language features suggest unspoken feelings?

Now read the commentary on pages 47–48.

(Serge has bought a modern painting for thousands of pounds. It is five foot by four, a white canvas with fine white diagonal scars. He is showing it to his friend Yvan.)

A long pause, while Yvan studies the painting and Serge studies Yvan.

YVAN:	Oh yes. Yes, yes.
SERGE:	Antrios.
YVAN:	Yes, yes.
SERGE:	It's a seventies Antrios. Worth mentioning. He's going through a similar phase now, but this one's from the seventies.
YVAN:	Yes, yes. Expensive?
SERGE:	In absolute terms, yes. In fact, no. You like it?
YVAN:	Oh, yes, yes, yes.
SERGE:	Plain.
YVAN:	Plain, yes ... Yes ... And at the same time ...
SERGE:	Magnetic.
YVAN:	Mm ... yes ...
SERGE:	You don't really get the resonance just at the moment.
YVAN:	Well, a bit ...
SERGE:	No, you don't. You have to come back in the middle of the day. That resonance you get from something monochromatic, it doesn't really happen under artificial light.
YVAN:	Mm hm.
SERGE:	Not that it is actually monochromatic.
YVAN:	No! ... How much was it?
SERGE:	Two hundred thousand.
YVAN:	Very reasonable.

The most common way of representing dialogue in prose is to use speech marks to identify the words spoken:

'What are you waiting for?'

and to add on an explanatory comment. This may be a plain identification of the speaker:

'he / she said'

The writer often interprets the tone of voice by using a **synonym** for 'said' that includes the manner of speaking:

'he / she shouted / whispered / complained, etc.'

This authorial comment can go further by adding **adverbs**, such as 'gently', or adverbial **phrases**, such as 'with surprise / in an outraged voice'.

When prose writers represent dialogue, there is a range of authorial comment. Romantic novels like those published by Mills & Boon give a lot of interpretation. You should recognise the following example as a parody of this style of romantic fiction: it repeats the familiar pattern of synonym for 'said' plus adverb, in an unvarying way. The search for different **verbs** and adverbs seems forced and, in this case, ridiculously inappropriate to the mundane subject matter.

	Pronoun	Verb	Adverb
'Good morning,'	she	ventured	diffidently.
'Morning,'	he	grunted	tersely.
'Your car's a 2CV, isn't it?'	she	reminded	pungently.
'That's right,'	he	agreed	laconically.
'Is it orange?'	she	added	dulcetly.
'I know what you're going to say,'	he	interjected	enigmatically.

At the other end of the spectrum, writers like James Joyce and Roddy Doyle use a technique that is close to a play script, with very little authorial interpretation or comment.

– Where you going?

– Town. What about you?

ACTIVITY 12

Read the following extracts and assess the representation of dialogue on a scale of 1–10. 1 signifies minimal interpretation and comment from the author and 10 signifies the highest level of authorial comment.

Now read the commentary on page 48.

EXTRACT 1 (WAR ANTHOLOGY: FROM TEXT 3 *HARPER'S WEEKLY*, 2 JUNE 1864)

'Is it Olive?' he asked eagerly ... 'I knew you were there,' he said; 'I heard your voice, and it was better than a whole bottle of wine to me.'

'You knew I was here, and yet waited without calling to me?' Olive said reproachfully.

'You couldn't have come to me without leaving others, you know,' he said, gently.

The girl's only answer was a kiss and a sob; and then she said to me, 'It is my cousin, Philip.'

'Of course it is, Olive,' I said, 'and it is time he was removed to the hospital.'

She got up then, blushing deeply as she saw the men waiting with a litter – waiting with a respectful, sympathetic look, that spoke plainly enough their appreciation of the scene.

EXTRACT 2 (WAR ANTHOLOGY: FROM TEXT 4 *A FAREWELL TO ARMS*, BY ERNEST HEMINGWAY, 1929)

'Shoot him if he resists,' an officer said. 'Take him over back.'

'Who are you?'

'You'll find out.'

'Who are you?'

'Battle police,' another officer said.

'Why don't you ask me to step over instead of having one of these airplanes grab me?'

They did not answer. They did not have to answer. They were battle police.

'Take him back there with the others,' the first officer said. 'You see, he speaks Italian with an accent.'

'So do you, you bastard,' I said.

'Take him back with the others,' the first officer said.

Purpose and audience

This aspect of the discourse of the text concentrates on the relationship between the author of the text and the intended audience. The **purpose** of the text is one important aspect that influences the use of language. An account of a wartime incident may be to provide information, or it may have a persuasive purpose. It may, of course, *appear* to give factual information, but be slanted towards a particular viewpoint. In films and novels about war, there is the additional need to entertain by engaging the emotions, whether horror or excitement. It is usually possible to identify a mixture of purposes and it is interesting to notice an underlying purpose, as well as the apparent purpose of the text.

The intended **audience** is another important aspect that influences the use of language. Language is sometimes used in a private context, for example a conversation, a letter or e-mail to a friend, diary entries. If the writer knows that a letter or diary entry may have a wider audience, there may be more careful manipulation of the language. On the other hand, a text crafted for a wide audience may try to create the impression of a private, spontaneous use of language. It is interesting to notice if there is a difference between the apparent audience and the actual audience. In the Alan Bennett monologues, for example, the speakers are apparently talking aloud to themselves or perhaps confiding in one close friend, though the actual audience is television viewers. Some charity letters use a typeface that looks like handwriting and address the reader as a personal friend.

ACTIVITY 13

The genre of the first text is an extract from an essay; the second text is a magazine editorial.

- Read each and comment on the purposes – apparent and underlying.
- Do you feel that you are part of the intended audience for each text?
- What would the effect be on the intended audience?
- Identify some language features that seem significant to the achievement of either purpose or audience. Use linguistic terminology to describe these features, if possible.

Now read the commentary on page 48.

EXTRACT 1 (*Shooting an Elephant*, by George Orwell)
(The elephant had killed a man.)

When I pulled the trigger I did not hear the bang or feel the kick – one never does when a shot goes home – but I heard the devilish roar of glee that went up from the crowd. In that instant, in too short a time, one would have thought, even for the bullet to get there, a mysterious, terrible change had come over the elephant. He neither stirred nor fell, but every line of his body had altered. He looked suddenly stricken, shrunken, immensely old, as though the frightful impact of the bullet had paralysed him without knocking him down. At last, after what seemed a long time – it might have been five seconds, I dare say – he sagged flabbily to his knees. His mouth slobbered. An enormous senility seemed to have settled upon him. One could have imagined him thousands of years old.

EXTRACT 2 (Editorial in *Bliss*)

Welcome to the latest, brightest, most brilliant edition of *Bliss*. And have we got a top issue for you! Firstly, have you checked out our hair book? It's designed to make sure that even though you're probably back in daggy college gear, your hair will still be on top form. And just to make sure your life is a back-to-school depression-free zone,

Bliss' Jo and Jenny have been scouring the world for seven of the most babelicious new boys we could find.

On a sadder note, our Art Ed, Bill, has left to become a currazy freelance designer – so good luck Bill! But it's hallo to Phil Chill, our cool, new office DJ (and sub) who's been playing loads of ace toons to keep the office rockin'.

Enjoy the issue.

Dawn

ACTIVITY 14   C3.2

Classify the texts in the anthology according to **a)** purpose and **b)** audience.

Expect to find a mixture of purposes, rather than a simple one-word definition.

Look out for texts that have a specific, limited audience. You may decide that poetry and fiction have a wide, general audience.

No commentary.

Historical and social context

The term 'context' refers to the situation in which the text was produced. So far you have looked at the aspect of mode – whether the text was originally spoken or written and whether it was written to be listened to or read. Then you looked at the aspect of purpose and audience. Other important aspects of context are the time and place.

You will notice from the dates that the texts in the anthology come from a variety of periods in history. The historical context in which the text was produced is significant. In the case of an anthology of texts about war, for example, there may be a sense of patriotic fervour just before war is declared, but this may change once the horrific consequences are felt.

The social context may also be significant. Some writers were involved in the fighting; others write from the point of view of a civilian, worrying about absent relatives. A woman's viewpoint on war is likely to be significantly different from that of a man.

ACTIVITY 15

Note the dates of each text in your anthology. This will give one aspect of the context in which each text was written.

What other aspects of the social context do you notice? Think about the gender, social and regional background of the writers. Are there writers from countries other than the UK?

No commentary.

Attitudes and values

The skills required in the study of English Language and Literature range from relatively straightforward – identify, describe, comment – to more sophisticated – analyse, interpret, respond. As well as being able to *identify* the context, you need to 'show understanding of the ways contextual variation shapes the meaning of texts'. The attitudes and values expressed are likely to reflect the social and historical contexts of the texts. These may be explicit (stated clearly) or implicit (inferred by 'reading between the lines'). As the reader, you may *respond* by accepting the implicit values and attitudes or by resisting them. Some examples of 'resistant readings' of texts follow.

Some images reflect the values and attitudes of a particular cultural context. A visitor to the UK was shocked by the amount of freedom women have in the British culture and explained:

'My wife is like gold. I keep her safe in a box.'

This example illustrates the difference there can be between the attitude *created* and the attitude *conveyed*. The speaker intended to create a positive image, suggesting how precious the woman is and the respect and concern with which he treats her. The listener, however, might interpret the image in negative terms, the woman being presented as a possession that needs to be locked away. These are two very different interpretations of what the image meant.

When you read texts from contexts different from your own, you are likely to notice differences in the attitudes implied, or stated explicitly. Many traditional stories, for example, are based on the values and attitudes of the time, some of which may conflict with your own values and attitudes. The ultimate goal for young women in many traditional stories is to marry the prince. Stepmothers are always evil; the youngest child succeeds despite the trickery of the older siblings. In the tale of Cinderella, we may approve of the way a poor, downtrodden girl succeeds in the end, but not be so happy with the notion that small feet are better than large! This may seem trivial, yet the binding of girl babies' feet to stunt their growth shows that this attitude has had some lasting influence. In Western cultures, people undergo major cosmetic surgery in order to conform to the perceived ideal of human beauty. Two of Shakespeare's plays attract controversy when they are staged today, yet may not have attracted any comment at the time: *The Merchant of Venice* has some disturbing assumptions about Jews in the portrayal of Shylock and *The Taming of the Shrew* delights in the way the feisty young woman, Kate, is subdued into willing obedience once she marries.

ACTIVITY 16

Read the following extract from a brochure advertising a school of grooming and deportment. It was published in the 1980s.

- What values and attitudes are expressed?

- Write down some of the implicit assumptions of the text: 'The text assumes that ...'

- Are you a resistant reader of this text?

Now read the commentary on page 49.

When a girl reaches adolescence she enters quite a different world and has to find her own place in it. For the first time she is acting on her own initiative and often feels insecure and inadequate. Often she has undiscovered potential which is of the greatest importance to her, which enables her to overcome her insecurity and uncertainty. Whatever age we are, at certain stages in our lives, we may suffer from a lack of confidence which makes us feel insecure, and sometimes even afraid. This can be particularly devastating if we are looking for a first job, change of occupation or starting a new life. We all need a helping hand to find ourselves to overcome our shyness and develop our gifts. Life can start or begin at any age. The ONE DAY SEMINAR we recommend can do just this.

It will give us poise, and self-assurance, because we will be confident that we know how to behave in any circumstances. When our clothes and make-up are right and our deportment is good, we feel able to meet people at any level.

The day seminar includes:

A LECTURE AND DEMONSTRATION on skin care and make-up technique

ADVICE ON NUTRITION and body care is also given and special diets are recommended to anyone on request

POSTURE AND DEPORTMENT, sitting, standing, walking and how to remove and put on outer garments easily, smoothly and elegantly

HOW TO ENTER AND LEAVE a room correctly, how to ascend and descend stairs, also getting in and out of a car gracefully.

Bridging the gap

The activities so far have concentrated on the large issues involved when reading texts:

- genre
- perspective
- purpose and audience
- historical and social context
- values and attitudes.

The commentaries have identified some words and phrases as evidence of the *ways* in which these issues are dealt with in a text. Very little terminology has been used up to this point. In your exam answers, you should give a sensitive interpretation of the text, provide evidence from the text *and* be able to use the appropriate terminology to describe the language features. In Activity 16, for example, the term **pronoun** would accurately pinpoint the shift from 'she' to 'we'; the term 'negative connotations' would highlight the significant choice of words like 'insecurity', 'suffer', 'afraid', 'devastating'.

The following activities move back down the hierarchy of language levels to examine and describe features of phonology, lexis and grammar. (Morphology and graphology will be referred to in Module 2 and Module 3.)

The nuts and bolts of language

Although it might seem logical to begin with the smallest units and gradually build up, the level of lexis is the most accessible. Lexis refers to choice of words, vocabulary or diction. It is not important which of the terms you choose to use. The term 'vocabulary' or 'word' has been used so far, as these are more familiar.

The words

One way to analyse the words used in a text is to label the **word class** that it belongs to. Most grammar books agree that there are seven or eight different types of word. The words that convey most of the content are:

- nouns
- verbs
- adjectives
- adverbs.

The grammatically useful words are:

- pronouns
- prepositions
- determiners
- conjunctions.

Being able to say whether something is a noun or a verb is a source of pride to those who can do it and a source of embarrassment to those who worry that they can't. Labelling word classes can be boring, if it is done with a train-spotting mentality, where simply adding more numbers to the list is the ultimate goal. But it can be fascinating and revealing.

Nouns and verbs

What is a **noun**? Most people remember their junior-school definition: 'A noun is a naming word.' This only works for the obvious, classic nouns. It is much more reliable to think of the way that nouns function in a sentence. Nouns are the type of words that can be preceded by **determiners** like 'the _____ / a _____ / my _____', and this is a useful test for tricky cases like this example:

A student of English asked the author, 'What is a must?' I was stuck for a quick answer and finally asked the student to give the whole sentence. It was a poster advertising Windsor Castle that had the slogan 'Windsor Castle is a Must!' Although the common use of 'must' is as a verb, as in 'I must go', it was being used as a noun.

Word classes are very flexible in English. The word 'torpedo' is used as a noun in phrases like 'the torpedo', but it can be used as a verb in phrases like 'A submarine torpedoed the destroyer.' You recognise that new, unfamiliar or nonsense words are being used as verbs, even if you don't know what they mean. Verbs occur in contexts like this:

- Don't criteria me. *don't (verb)*

- She was shuggling up. *(verb) + 'ing'*

- I galumphed out. *(verb) + 'ed'*

- It is a crime to blaspheme. *to (verb)*

ACTIVITY 17

- As you sit in the classroom, notice anything you can put a name to in a phrase that begins with the words 'the / a / my'. The second word is a noun.

- Make a list of about twenty nouns.

- Can you use any of these words as verbs? Try putting the word in a phrase like 'I'm going to _____' or any of the four structures listed above.

Now read the commentary on page 49.

Types of noun

Any labelling system gets more and more complex in the quest to label everything precisely. There are many sub-categories of nouns: concrete v. abstract, proper v. common, mass v. count.

There is not space in this book to explore all these categories. In any case, it is more important to avoid pointless feature-spotting. The ability to label with the correct terminology is only a tool, but a tool that needs to be used well. Begin with intuition, 'This looks interesting / unusual' and then explore further, until you can say what is unusual and why it is interesting.

First a brief definition of one type of noun: *proper nouns* refer to names of people, products, places, institutions and are written with capital letters. This **graphological** feature makes proper nouns easy to identify, but is it ever interesting to point out that a text contains proper nouns?

ACTIVITY 18

Read the following extract from Chapter 18 of the novel *Glamorama*, by Bret Easton Ellis.

- Note the number of proper nouns used.

- Is this significant? What is the effect of using so many proper nouns?

Now read the commentary on page 49.

At Conrad's loft on Bond Street it's 1:30 which is really the only time to practice since everyone else in the building is at work or at Time Café acting like an idiot without trying over lunch, and from where I slouch in the doorway leading into the loft I can see all the members of the Impersonators lying around in various positions, each next to his own amp: Aztec's wearing a Hang-10 T-shirt, scratching at a Kenny Scharf tattoo on his bicep, Fender in lap; Conrad, our lead singer, has a kind of damp appeal and dated Jenny McCarthy and has wilted hair the color of lemonade and dresses in rumpled linens; Fergy's wrapped in an elongated cardigan and playing with a Magic 8 Ball, sunglasses lowered; and Fitzgerald was in a gothic rock band, OD'd, was resuscitated, OD'd again, was resuscitated again, campaigned mindlessly for Clinton, modeled for Versace, dated Jennifer Capriati, and he's wearing pyjamas and sleeping in a giant hot-pink-and-yucca-striped beanbag chair. And they're all existing in this freezing, screwy-looking loft where DAT tapes and CDs are scattered everywhere, MTV's on, Presidents of the United States merging into a Mentos commercial merging into an ad for the new Jackie Chan movie, empty Zen Palate take-out boxes are strewn all over the place, white roses dying in an empty Stoli bottle, a giant sad ragdoll photo by Mike Kelly dominates one wall, the collected works of Philip K. Dick fill an entire row in the room's only bookcase, Lava lamps, cans of Play-Doh.

Pronouns

A pronoun stands in for a noun, hence the name 'pro-noun'. Any noun phrase can be replaced by a pronoun: **1st person**, **2nd person** or **3rd person**. For example, 'My best friend, Helen, from Junior School got married' can be expressed as, 'She got married'. Pronouns are thus often used to avoid repetition. A simple scheme is produced below:

	Singular	plural	?
1st person	I	we	one
2nd person	you	you	
3rd person	he, she, it	they	

However, there are some interesting gaps and overlaps in the English pronoun system.

The pronoun 'you' can refer to one person or many, to a friend or to a polite acquaintance. The single term replaces 'thee', 'thou' and 'ye' in older forms of English – and some regional dialects. Other languages have ways of distinguishing singular and plural ('tu' and 'vous' in French), friendly and polite address ('tu' and 'lei' in Italian). This means that English needs to use other ways of signalling degrees of intimacy and politeness.

The pronoun 'he' refers to a male; 'she' to a female and 'it' to most non-humans – things and animals – but not, interestingly to ships, countries and even cars. 'They' refers to any plural group. There is no term that refers to a single person regardless of gender. This causes problems if a writer is trying to avoid specifying the gender. (See page 130.)

The pronoun 'one' can be used in this non-specific sense: 'One should always doff one's cap to a lady.' But its use in modern English is restricted to formal contexts such as debating speeches or essays: 'If one considers the rise in unemployment ...'

The pronoun 'we' does not necessarily refer to the speakers. 'What are we doing today?' could be spoken by one friend referring to the whole group, or by a doctor referring to one other person.

The choice of pronouns was significant in the text studied in Activity 16. It is often interesting to identify and interpret the pronoun use in texts.

ACTIVITY 19

Read the poem 'Strange Meeting', by Wilfred Owen.

- Pick out the key words in the line: 'I am the enemy you killed, my friend.'

- Use the terms 'noun', 'verb' and 'pronoun' to describe the class of each word in this line.

- Represent the links and contrasts between the words diagrammatically.

- What are the possible interpretations of the meaning of this line?

Now read the commentary on pages 49–50.

STRANGE MEETING

It seemed that out of battle I escaped
Down some profound dull tunnel, long since scooped
Through granites which titanic wars had groined.

Yet also there encumbered sleepers groaned,
Too fast in thought or death to be bestirred.
Then, as I probed them, one sprang up, and stared
With piteous recognition in fixed eyes,

Lifting distressful hands, as if to bless.
And by his smile, I knew that sullen hall, –
By his dead smile I knew we stood in Hell.

With a thousand pains that vision's face was grained;
Yet no blood reached there from the upper ground,
And no guns thumped, or down the flues made moan.
'Strange friend,' I said, 'here is no cause to mourn.'
'None,' said that other, 'save the undone years,
The hopelessness. Whatever hope is yours,
Was my life also; I went hunting wild
After the wildest beauty in the world,
Which lies not calm in eyes, or braided hair,
But mocks the steady running of the hour,
And if it grieves, grieves richlier than here.
For by my glee might many men have laughed,
And of my weeping something had been left,
Which must die now. I mean the truth untold,
The pity of war, the pity war distilled.
Now men will go content with what we spoiled,
Or, discontent, boil bloody, and be spilled.
They will be swift with swiftness of the tigress.
None will break ranks, though nations trek from progress.
Courage was mine, and I had mystery,
Wisdom was mine, and I had mastery:
To miss the march of this retreating world
Into vain citadels that are not walled.
Then, when much blood had clogged their chariot-wheels,
I would go up and wash them from sweet wells,
Even with truths that lie too deep for taint.
I would have poured my spirit without stint
But not through wounds; not on the cess of war.
Foreheads of men have bled where no wounds were.
I am the enemy you killed, my friend.
I knew you in this dark: for so you frowned
Yesterday through me as you jabbed and killed.
I parried; but my hands were loath and cold.
Let us sleep now ...'

Adjectives

An **adjective** is commonly defined as 'a describing word'. This is actually very misleading, as many types of words are descriptive in some way. Take the following sentence, for example:

> The drunk tottered into the alley clutching a bottle of vodka under his raincoat.

Many of the words are descriptive, but there isn't a single adjective. A more reliable way of identifying adjectives is to look at the way the word functions in a sentence. Adjectives are commonly used before nouns or after the verb 'to be':

> The small, fluffy kitten.
> The kitten is small and fluffy.

Adjectives can sometimes be altered to show comparative or superlative qualities:

> small, smallest
> more fluffy, most fluffy (or fluffier, fluffiest?)

Unlike nouns and verbs, adjectives are optional extras. It can be interesting to notice whether a writer uses adjectives sparingly or lavishly. The effect depends partly on your taste, as you will see in Activity 20.

Adverbs

Adverbs are also optional extras. Their name indicates that they often function to give more information about a verb – how, when or where it happened:

> She stepped quietly / determinedly / downstairs / immediately.

You will notice that adverbs are often formed from adjectives by adding '-ly', but there are many exceptions to this rule.

However, adverbs also have two other functions, which can be more interesting for style. One is to intensify adjectives, so they are sometimes referred to as intensifiers:

The kitten is	very	fluffy.
	extremely	
	amazingly	
	hugely	
	gorgeously	

The list can be extended by as many suitable adjectives as you can think of. These words don't express degrees of intensity very precisely, but they can convey impressions of the speaker, as Activity 20 shows.

The other function of adverbs is to indicate the attitude of the speaker to what they are saying. In the sentence, 'The referee was allegedly bribed', the adverb can come first, at the end, or in the middle of the statement.

Allegedly, the referee was bribed.
The referee was bribed, allegedly.
The referee was allegedly bribed.

ACTIVITY 20

- Identify the adjectives and adverbs in the following passage. (Nouns are in bold; verbs are underlined.)

- Which ones can be omitted?

- What is the effect of removing or keeping the extra descriptive words?

Now read the commentary on page 50.

Time stood still as the rosy red **ribbon** of early morning **sunlight** stretched lazily over the dusty **scrubland** below us. A blurry **haze** was already rising above the scorched yellow **stubble**, threatening an oppressive and overbearing **heat**. **Families** of elegant **impala**, **kudu** and **eland** were grazing peacefully on the sparse **vegetation** below, their **predators** already having taken refuge in the little **shelter** they could find. Lolling idly in the withered **turf**, their dusty golden **bodies** were cleverly camouflaged.

ACTIVITY 21

- What do the following choices of intensifier suggest about the speaker (or writer)?

- Do some suggest a particular age group, social class or gender?

It was	awfully	good.
	jolly	
	really	
	incredibly	
	dead	
	right	
	well	

And a few taboo words:

It was	damn	good.
	bloody	
	xxxxing	

No commentary.

Semantics

Semantics is the study of words and their meanings. Important concepts are:

- **figurative language**
- connotation
- **collocation**
- etymology
- **semantic field**.

Literary terminology

These are some useful terms for analysing types of figurative language, or imagery.

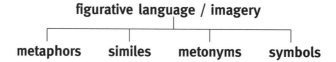

There is a distinction between these terms, but they often overlap, so it is not always possible to say exactly which category an image falls into.

There are thousands of words in the English language, but an infinite number of experiences and feelings. In the struggle to express sensations for which there are no simple words, we use the existing store of words in figurative ways.

People sometimes assume that only literature uses figurative language. You should be aware of how much figurative language is used in non-literary as well as literary texts. The words 'twisted' or 'coiled' originally describe the physical quality of something like wire, which is bent tightly – no longer straight. Words like 'straightforward' suggest **abstract** qualities of honesty and simplicity. When we describe a person, their feelings or actions as 'twisted', the mental process involves a form of comparison, usually between something physical and an abstract concept. The terms image or 'imagery' refer to this use of language.

Similes make the comparison explicit, often by using words such as 'like' or 'as':

> Her emotions were coiled like a spring.

Metaphors suggest a comparison by referring to one thing in terms of another. The expression 'you're winding me up' invites comparison between an emotional state and coiled wire; extending the comparison suggests not only the tension of the coiled state but the likelihood of it springing apart.

Sometimes the phrase is so familiar that the image loses its impact, in which case it is can be called a 'dead' metaphor, or a cliché. The simile 'sick as a parrot' must have been striking the first time it was used. Trying to imagine how the tiny throat of a parrot would cope with vomiting is shocking or hilarious, depending on your viewpoint.

Andrew Rissik wrote, 'Great literature always internalises its landscapes: it turns the physical world into a mirror of the mind's private affliction.' (The *Guardian*, 22 April 2000) But this does not just happen in literature; metaphors and similes are a feature of everyday language as well as literature. In *Metaphors We Live By* by George Lakoff, Lakoff points out the large number of metaphors in everyone's language use. The spatial concepts of 'up' and 'down', 'in front' and 'behind' are used to convey a range of feelings and attitudes. The term 'literal' is used for their primary sense and metaphorical for their extended sense. So 'pick yourself up' does not literally mean that you raise yourself off the ground, nor does 'I'm feeling down' mean that you are physically near the ground. We also use related images in terms like 'depressed', 'low' and 'uplifted' or 'on top of the world'. Activity 22 asks you to collect some of the metaphors you live by.

ACTIVITY 22

In small groups, pick one of these pairs of physical concepts and think of metaphors and similes using these concepts. You do not always have to use the word itself.

heavy – light
inside – outside
hard – soft
dark – light
cold – hot

Now read the commentary on pages 50–51, which offers some examples.

The choice of figurative language can reveal the attitudes and values of the particular culture or writer. It is important to make these underlying assumptions explicit, in order to understand the range of meanings in the text. If a type of criminal behaviour is described as a 'cancer', for example, that implies the need for it to be cut out.

ACTIVITY 23

Read the following letter written to a problem page and its reply (1997).

• List the metaphors used and try to find connected images.

• What do they suggest about the way this society sees love and relationships?

• Think of other images that are used in song lyrics, articles and conversations about love.

Now read the commentary on page 51.

My guy's leaving me

I've been dating an older boy for about a year (I'm 16 and he's 18). The age difference has meant nothing to us – until now. You see, he's off to university this autumn, which means we'll have to split up. I reckon we could still carry on seeing each other, but he says it's best to end it, rather than letting things drag on any longer. Is this just his way of dumping me?

Carol, Liverpool

For many, going to university is a major step 'cause it's symbolic of gaining independence.

Of course, some find it hard, so they keep relationships at home going to give them something to run back to. But your boyfriend is trying to sever these links before he goes. It's a brave move on his part, and an honest one. He could let things tick over and just fizzle out, but instead he's making a clean break now. It's hard, but I think you should accept his decision. If you kept it going, you may be let down less kindly later on.

I know it hurts, but breaking up now will be less painful than being unsure about what he's up to when he's away. My advice is to let him go.

You have seen that metaphors and similes involve an element of comparison. Images are often used without such explicit comparison.

Colours are a clear example of **symbols**. Red stands for danger or stop in traffic lights, and green stands for go. Because red is the colour of blood, there may be a natural connection, but the choice of green seems arbitrary. There is no obvious connection between the colour green and what it stands for, nor between green and jealousy. Symbols often vary from culture to culture. Black is the colour of death and mourning in our culture, but white clothes are worn to funerals in Eastern cultures.

The term **metonym** is used for images where a part of something stands for the whole. A 'private eye' is a type of detective, but the image of the eye represents the occupation – although it probably involves a lot more filing of papers and hanging about at railway stations, than looking at clues through a magnifying glass. We often use metonyms in everyday language, when we characterise types of people by referring to one aspect of their appearance: for example, anorak or medallion man. The use of metonyms in this way relies on stereotyping and is bound up with the attitudes and values of a particular society. The artist, Tracy Emin, caused a lot of controversy with her work shortlisted for the Turner Prize in 1999. It was an unmade bed strewn with objects that she used to express something about her life and feelings. Language, as well as visual art, also uses images in this way.

ACTIVITY 24

List some other symbols. You might start with national symbols on flags, other colours, the sun and moon, a circle and a square.

Describe the bedroom of a character / person, picking out objects and features that can be interpreted as metonyms. You might include specific CDs, ornaments, pictures on the walls.

No commentary.

Denotation v. connotation

There are many words that are 'loaded'. They do not simply describe something, but also indicate the attitude towards it. The **denotation** of a word is its literal, dictionary definition. The *connotations* of a word are the associations that it creates. Connotations might be individual or cultural. 'Terrorist', 'guerrilla' and 'freedom fighter' have similar denotations, but different connotations. This is one reason for saying that there are no exact synonyms in a language. There may be a number of near synonyms, each denoting a similar quality, but having different connotations. The following list, for example, denotes a below-average physical build. Apart from indicating degrees of positive–neutral–negative connotations, some of the words are more associated with female qualities, others are less commonly used and so sound more elegant or posh. For this reason, it is misleading to say that such words are exact synonyms – as no two words mean exactly the same. You could add phrases, such as 'sylph-like' or 'skin and bone' and lengthen the list.

> petite
> slim
> slender
> slight
> thin
> lean
> lanky
> skinny
> emaciated
> anorexic

Positive connotations outnumber the negative with this quality. This need not be the case, as you may find in Activity 25.

ACTIVITY 25

- List words denoting above-average build.

- Use a thesaurus to add to the list.

- Group them, starting with the most neutral denotation and moving to the positive and negative.

No commentary.

Collocation

Collocation means 'locating with' and refers to the fact that words tend to occur in a particular context with others. 'Gambol' means a skipping movement, but only lambs gambol, for example. The word gambol virtually never occurs with any other living creature. This aspect of word use also makes it tricky to say that two words are exact synonyms. 'Strong' and 'powerful' may seem like synonyms, but they occur in different collocations. Arguments can be described as either strong or powerful. Tea can be strong, but not powerful. A car can be powerful but not strong. The collocation of a word affects its connotation, as Activity 26 shows.

ACTIVITY 26

- Write down as many phrases as you can think of that include the word 'common'.

- Look up 'common' in a dictionary. You will find several slightly different uses defined.

- Note any collocations suggested, e.g. 'common noun'.

- Decide whether each has positive, negative or fairly neutral connotations for you.

Now read the commentary on page 51.

Etymology

Etymology is concerned with the historical origins of words. Any dictionary large enough not to fit into a slim pocket shows the origins of each word in square brackets at the end of the definition. This might sound a dry subject, but it can be fascinating, especially when it shows how meanings have developed or changed. The word 'insult' for example comes from a Latin word meaning to leap on. 'Nice' originally meant stupid, from the Latin word meaning ignorant.

ACTIVITY 27

Read the following comment from a speaker on the radio.

- How do you react to the implied values?

- How were they constructed?

- Pick out the adjectives and other descriptive phrases.

- What are the usual collocations and the connotations of 'wallowing'?

- Look up the etymology of 'vulgar' in a dictionary.

Now read the commentary on page 52.

> Blackpool is vulgar. The sea and beach are dirty, the amusement arcades are ugly and the people are unpleasant. People are wallowing – there is no other word for it – in litter. Their idea of fun is to wear false breasts and drop their trousers for photographers from the *Daily Mail.*

Semantic field

If you are reading a recipe or a menu, it is not surprising to find a number of words from the field of food. However, you might also find words from other fields of meaning, for example '*nestling* on a *bed* of lettuce ... *cradled* in a *cushion* of mashed potato'. Each of the words in italics is used in a figurative sense, so the occurrence of related words can be called an **extended metaphor**. This is the more usual literary term, whereas 'semantic field' is the linguistic term for the same concept.

Whatever you decide to call it, such unusual fields of meaning are significant to the effect of the text. The menu is suggesting the comfort that food can give. The choice of semantic field creates implied meanings and attitudes. Money, for example, is often referred to in terms of living organisms: watch your money grow, your investment matures, your family flourishes. In some societies children are seen as valuable commodities to help with work and to care for elderly parents. This attitude to children is seen in the commonly used phrase, 'He has produced two children.' The words used in computer technology are often noticeably ordinary terms from the field of the home and the office – windows, menu, tools. Because of this avoidance of **jargon**, more people may feel comfortable using computers.

ACTIVITY 28

- Read the following list of words and try to guess the topic of the full text.

- Group the words into two or more semantic fields.

   Orders ... cut ... shots ... smoking ... Embassy ... it is being claimed ... pressure group ... has launched an all-out attack ... policy ... headless torsos, disembodied legs and unidentifiable buttocks ... instruction followed an initiative ... cut down ... number of shots ... smoking ... under a great deal of pressure ... spokesman denied ... in a nutcracker here ... in the middle of a very difficult situation.

Now read the commentary on page 52.

The grammar

It is useful to be able to analyse and describe sentence structure, as well as to comment on the choice of individual words. You can do this in two ways. First notice whether a sentence is making a statement, asking a question, giving an instruction or making an exclamation. The following terms are used to describe the four main sentence types.

1 declarative, or statements

2 interrogative, or questions

3 imperative, or commands

4 exclamations.

A fifth sentence type, echoes, is sometimes referred to, but this almost never occurs in writing.

The first term describes the structure and the second its usual function. It does not matter which you prefer to use. It is more important to make comments that are significant, than simply to spot sentence types. However, remember that the structure of the sentence may not be the same as its function. This is the level of pragmatics, where the implied meaning may not match the surface meaning. In the following examples, the structures are shown in italics and the implied meanings in brackets.

Declaratives are the norm for stretches of language, so it is more interesting to comment on the use of other sentence types. However, statements may be used, particularly in spoken language, to encourage others to act:

It's rather cold in here. (Please close the window.)

Why do people watch soap operas? **Interrogative** structures are easy to identify. In written language the verb always comes before the subject and the sentence ends with a question mark. In spoken language, a question can be signalled by tone of voice, so it is not always necessary to change the order of the subject and verb:

(are) You going to the shops?

The function of questions is not necessarily to ask for information:

Are you going to the shops or what? (Please hurry up and go to the shops.)

Imperatives use the simple form of the verb without any pronoun:

Join a club. Don't be afraid.

Speakers and writers can soften a command by using a modal verb: 'You could join a club'. Direct commands are often avoided if the speaker wishes to be polite, as seen in the question structures used as indirect commands: 'Can you lend me a fiver?'

Although there may be exclamation marks at the end of sentences, this does not mean that the structure is an exclamation. These are like inverted questions, beginning with 'What' or 'How', and are quite rare in written language:

What a fantastic idea that is! (What is a fantastic idea?)
How lovely you look! (How do you look lovely?)

In spoken language, single words can be used as exclamations: *No! Alas! Oh!* The use of exclamation marks after a statement makes it more emphatic, although it is not strictly an exclamation, for example 'It's so hot in here!'

Echoes are common in spoken language, where one speaker repeats all or part of the previous utterance. This use of language has various functions. It can express surprise, be used to query, agree or confirm, depending on the context. The way it is said usually makes it clear.

> I didn't want to go.
> *You didn't want to go.*

Conversations (whether originally spoken or fictional dialogue) are interactive, so are likely to use a number of questions, commands, exclamations and echoes. If these occur in a written text such as a leaflet, it creates a sense of interaction.

ACTIVITY 29

Read the following transcript of a conversation between a stallholder (SH) at a fairground and some boys.

- Identify any questions, commands, exclamations or echoes.

- How do you interpret the functions of each type of sentence?

Now read the commentary on pages 52–53.

SH:	You having a go boys ... see what you can nick ... can I show you this one before you go ... no money ... show you this one mate ... no money we don't charge owt to listen ... before you go speak to me
BOY A:	I might as well ... how much is it
SH:	It's a dead easy game mate ... it's 50p mate ... you get three shots ... all you've got to do mate is knock over the golf tee to get a prize ... if you lose mate ... that's it are you having a go
BOY A:	Yeah
SH:	Mate's not having a go as well
BOY B:	No
BOY C:	Got no cash
BOY B:	Got no dosh
BOY A:	Can you put it anywhere
SH:	Anywhere in that D mate
BOY B:	Chalk your ... chalk your thingy mate
SH:	Yeah chalk the cue first ... that's it ... that's the best idea ... where you from boys

BOY A:	Middlesborough
SH:	Middlesborough ... so you just here for the day
BOY A:	No we've been playing a football tournament
SH:	You've been playing football ... Lytham St Annes
BOYS:	Yeah
SH:	I see ... who you playing today
BOY B:	Rad ... Radcliffe
SH:	Radcliffe
BOY C:	Two Scottish teams
SH:	Two Scottish teams ... I see ... you sure you're not going to have a try ... see what you can do
BOY C:	I've no money

Sentence structure

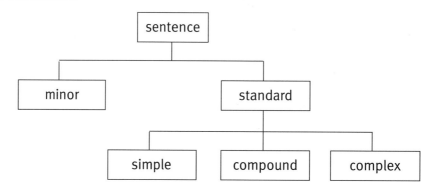

Most sentences have the structure of statements. There are four main types of sentence structure:

1 **simple** sentences, with one verb group

2 **compound** sentences, clauses linked simply by 'and', 'but', 'or'

3 **complex** sentences, where there are subordinate clauses bound together by connectives such as 'that' 'which' 'if', etc., or verbs ending in '-ing' or '-ed'

4 **minor** sentences, which are fragments of complete structures.

Most texts use a combination of these structures, although a formal style would avoid minor sentences. It is therefore not significant to comment that there is a combination.

This sentence is complex, *as* it contains four clauses, *joined* by two **conjunctions** and a **non-finite verb**, *which* you can see in italics (see further page 81).

This sentence is compound *and* it has two clauses.

The occasional simple sentence is often a deliberate choice. It can be very effective. These three sentences are all simple.

The use of minor sentences is also a deliberate choice and worth commenting on:

And here are five examples. Having a wonderful time. Wish you were here. Long time, no see. But don't overdo it.

ACTIVITY 30

- Identify examples of each type of sentence structure in the following text. Conjunctions and linking verbs have been printed in bold to help you see the divisions between clauses. In English, the conjunction 'that' can sometimes be omitted.

- What genre do you think this extract comes from?

Now read the commentary on page 53.

> **Although** we spend about a third of our lives asleep, we know little of the nature of sleep **and** nothing of its purpose. Everyone, **including** those who say **that** they never dream, probably dreams during REM sleep. **But** a dream is only remembered **if** one wakes almost at once. The 'non-dreamers' are the people who sleep on. **If** they are deliberately woken up **when** their eyes are seen to be moving, they remember dreaming like everyone else.
>
> Only one thing is certain. Sleep is necessary. The desire to sleep is almost overwhelming after two or three days without sleep. The effect is like drunkenness, **but** the person can pull himself together **and** behave normally for short periods. Sleep deprivation is an effective technique of brainwashing.

Effect on style

Compound sentence structures are sometimes described as 'loose' or 'periodic'. Their use is associated with rather simple forms of language. They are a feature of a child's language development, for example. The word 'and' is usually the first conjunction (joining word) acquired. In spontaneous speech, most people use 'and' a lot. If you still have examples of your own writing from junior school, you will probably find many sentences using 'and'. Yet the development of writing skills involves learning other ways of constructing longer sentences.

Because of this 'background', the use of many compound sentences in literary texts is unusual and it is worth commenting on the effect.

ACTIVITY 31

Read this extract from Chapter 15 of the novel *Glamorama*, by Bret Easton Ellis.

- Identify the compound structures, i.e. the use of the conjunction 'and'.

- What do you notice about the graphology (punctuation marks)?

- What is the effect of using such structures?

Now read the commentary on page 53.

4:00. From my third-floor vantage the club hasn't been this bustling since its inception and tables are being set by handpicked busboys who just skateboarded in, waiters brandishing glasses and tablecloths and candles also set chairs around the tables and the carpets are being vacuumed by guys with shag haircuts and a couple of waitresses who arrived early are being photographed by shadowy clumps of people while dancers rehearse amid technicians and security teams and guest-list people and three gorgeous coat-check girls chew gum and flaunt their midriffs and pierced belly buttons and bars are being stocked and giant flower displays are in the process of being strategically lit and Matthew Sweet's 'We're the Same' is blaring and the metal detectors sit in place at the entrance waiting to be entered and I'm taking it all in blankly, considering fleetingly what it all means and also that being semi-famous is in itself difficult but since it's so cold in the club it's hard to stay still so I rush up two flights to the offices more relieved than I should be that everything's finally falling into place.

Sounds and patterning

Sounds do not mean anything on their own, so why is it important to study the use of sounds in language? Hearing a song is generally a much more powerful experience than reading the lyrics on a song sheet. Similarly, a live reading of a poem has more impact. Sounds create physical and emotional effects, *like causing goose bumps*. The rhythm is often the most powerful aspect of music – drum beats can invigorate an army, for example. This book cannot explore the why's and how's of rhythm, but other aspects of sound are examined in the following activities.

ACTIVITY 32

Try this five-minute challenge.

- Write down everything you have ever heard and can remember word for word. But, it must be *more* than ten words long. It must *not* be from poems, songs, nursery rhymes or adverts.

- See how many examples the full group has produced.

- Now do the same activity, but include extracts from poems, songs, nursery rhymes and adverts.

Keep these examples for analysis after the next section.

Now read the commentary on page 54.

Rhyme

The use of **rhyme** for end words in lines of poetry can be effective, though it is tricky to explain exactly what the effect is. We notice a repeated sound; it throws some emphasis on the two words and their possible connection and it may please the ear. The use of rhyme does not guarantee success, of course. The effect of obvious or forced rhymes can be irritating. Some poetry is dismissed as 'verse', partly because of the over-use of such rhymes. Wilfred Owen uses **half-rhymes** in 'Strange Meeting', for example (see page 24). The **vowel** sound is slightly different, rather than repeated. These occur in couplets (pairs of lines) throughout the poem: 'escaped ... scooped ... groined ... groaned'. The effect of these is subtle, as the reader may not notice the faint echo. Perhaps you didn't at a conscious level, particularly if you read the poem in your head, rather than out loud. If you read the poem aloud, you will notice that each couple of lines half-rhymes. Now look back at your own examples of memorable language and see whether rhyme is a feature.

The concept of **foregrounding** is used to describe the effect of bringing something to your attention, rather than remaining like background noise or wallpaper. It is suggested that this effect can be created by **parallelism** (creating patterns by repetition) or by **deviation** (breaking the usual pattern). The patterning has an effect in itself, and also in any break from the pattern. Any deviation from the norm is highlighted, or foregrounded. As well as commenting on patterns created, it is often interesting to comment on breaks in the pattern.

Alliteration, assonance and consonance

Repetition of **consonant** and vowel sounds also creates patterns. The terms for these types of repetition are **alliteration**, **assonance** and **consonance**. You may want to interrupt at this point, as one student did: 'What is this "alliteration"?' The definition was provided: alliteration is the repetition of initial sounds, for example 'body beautiful'. The student's irritated response was, 'I know what it is. But what's the point?' The question was a good challenge. The labelling of such features is straightforward, but the *effect* is subtle and difficult to explain in words. We can say that it tends to make the words stand out. They are foregrounded for our attention because of the unusual degree of repetition. We are encouraged to consider them further – whether they are related in meaning, for example. However, there is a tendency for people to make extreme claims for the effect of alliteration. Beware of saying things like, 'It makes the text flow ...', 'It makes the reader relaxed ...' or even 'It suggests the inherent impossibility of achieving true love ...'! Alliteration can often be accidental and unnoticed; it can sometimes be deliberate and obvious:

Alliteration Analysis at Uttoxeter University with Professor Peter Porter.

Here is a brief definition of the other two terms, but remember not to worry about labelling, unless you feel that there is a point! If you notice a feature and think it has a significant effect, then it is worth describing and commenting on. Repetition of sounds is the significant feature of all three terms. As with all jargon, the need for precision leads to a complex vocabulary to make tiny distinctions. Many people use the term 'alliteration' loosely to cover all types of repeated sounds, apart from rhyme.

Assonance is the resemblance of sound (either vowels or consonants) between two syllables in nearby words. This need not be the initial sound.

Consonance is a recurrence of similar-sounding consonants.

Notice whether these features are present in your own examples of memorable language.

Onomatopoeia

There is a degree of **onomatopoeia** in the sound of words, i.e. some words seem to resemble the thing referred to. The similarity is often only approximate, for example 'whisper', 'miaow'. English speakers believe that dogs say 'bow wow', but in Indonesia dogs say 'gong gong'. Notice that these words describe *sounds*. It would be unconvincing to suggest that words for qualities or emotions are truly onomatopoeic: 'blooming', 'sad'. Although we do perceive some sounds as 'harsh' and others as 'soft', this is impressionistic and usually depends on the meaning and context as well as the sound. In the phrase 'big, bold and brassy' you might perceive the repeated 'b' sounds as aggressive, but not in the phrase 'body beautiful'. One example that is often quoted as an example of onomatopoeia is the line from Tennyson's poem 'In Memoriam':

> 'the murmuring of innumerable bees'

This line is enjoyed for the way that it seems to imitate a warm, buzzing sound with its repetition of nasal 'm' and 'n' sounds. However, if you make a slight change to:

> 'the murdering of innumerable bees'

the warm, cosy feeling disappears!

It is important to be sensitive to sounds, but remember not to make extreme claims about the effects of certain sounds. An interesting area is that of invented words for new concepts, where the sounds are often chosen to suggest a certain quality. Look at brand names for sweets, for example Curly Wurly, Jelly Belly Beans, or names for cartoon characters, for example Wizbit.

The writers Lewis Carroll and Roald Dahl (texts in Module 2) invented names for imaginary creatures; the Bandersnatch and the Jabberwock; the Oompaloompas and the Snozberry. Some technical knowledge will help you make accurate claims about the effect.

ACTIVITY 33

Read the drafts and final version from the War anthology of 'Anthem for Doomed Youth', by Wilfred Owen.

- Comment on the changes made in the following extracts.

- Note changes to the sound qualities of words and the changes in meaning.

Now read the commentary on pages 54–55.

Even the title went through some changes:

Anthem	for	Dead	Youth
	to		
	for	Doomed	

These are the changes to the first lines:

What	minute-	bells	for	these	who die	so fast?
	passing-			you		in herds?
				these		as cattle?

Only the	solemn	anger	of	our	guns.
	monstrous			more	guns.
				the	guns.

Let the blind insolence of	iron mouths
Only the stuttering rifles'	rattled words
	rapid rattle

Exam technique

You will have two questions to answer in the exam:

- *one* concentrating on the central collection of poetry (Text 1) in the anthology

- *one* focusing on texts from the rest of the anthology, including one or more of your own choice.

However the questions are phrased, they will require you to deal with:

- the ways that attitudes and values are created

- the importance of context

- the description and interpretation of variation in meaning and form.

Your first task is to analyse the question carefully so that you do cover each aspect. If you leave out any part of the question, you will lose all the marks for that part. If you include things not asked for, you will have wasted some of your time. Use a pen to highlight:

- the texts you are to discuss

- the verbs telling you what you are to do

- the aspects of the texts' meaning that you must focus on

- the features of language you should analyse.

ACTIVITY 34

Analyse the example questions below for Module 1, highlighting the details mentioned above:

- write the verbs telling you what you are to do as a main heading

- list the texts you are to discuss in one column, adding your choice

- list the aspects of meaning in one column

- list language features in one column.

Now read the commentary on page 55.

1 Examine the ways in which Owen uses language to convey ideas, feelings, attitudes and values in 'Inspection' and 'Strange Meeting' and one other poem of your choice.

You should refer to the following in the course of your answer:

- the ways language varies according to the author's purposes
- how the language conveys attitudes and values.

2 Compare the ways in which writers tell stories in the following:

- *The Naval Sister's Tale*
- 'The Obituary of Captain Goodwin'
- one other text of your choice from the anthology.

Examine in particular the ways in which the form, style and vocabulary help to shape the meanings of texts.

Once you have analysed the question, you should notice that your essay answer needs to be concise and well-focused. The length of an exam essay is rarely more than 750 words – check how much you can write in an hour on this type of question. If you are dealing with two or three texts, you should devote an equal amount of space to each. A few hundred words does not allow you to comment on everything, so you must prioritise the most important points.

It is worth spending five minutes making notes. If you begin by brainstorming, you must then isolate the most relevant and significant comments you wish to make in your answer.

As you write up your answer, make sure that you support each claim by reference to the text. Sometimes a general reference is sufficient, for example a comment about the overall structure of the obituary: 'The opening paragraph gives details of his age and his main reason for fame.' This provides enough detail for the reader without quotation. When you make a more specific claim, however, you should include a quote in support: 'A detailed account of this episode follows, telling the story with some dramatic details to engage the reader's imagination: "<u>diving</u> down through a <u>hail</u> of anti-aircraft fire."' It is useful to highlight the significant language features – done by underlining here. Then you should try to make a further comment on these features: 'The use of such imagery is similar to a fictional account to make the episode vivid.' This approach can be summarised as three stages:

1 Make a claim relevant to the task / question.

2 Support the claim by reference to the text.

3 If you quote, comment on the significant features.

Commentaries

Activity 1

It is a public service advert, with the purpose of persuading people not to drive after drinking alcohol. Its audience must be in a car, probably driving. The picture catches the attention first – the child appears to be staring at you. The text is very brief, so you can take it in at a glance, but the significance isn't immediately clear. The first sentence appears to be addressed directly at you, but the question occurs, 'Why won't I ever sleep?' The text is a bit like a riddle. You have to work out the unsaid, implied meanings – you have, or at least a driver has, killed this girl in a road accident and will never be able to forget the horror of it. The two short lines resemble lines of poetry; the sentences balance each other in the way that poetry sometimes does. The only changes are the choice of words from 'you' to 'she' and 'sleep' to 'wake'. Sleeping and waking are opposite activities; however, each has a metaphorical sense connected with death and life. Leaving the actual message till the end, and putting it in small print, means that the reader has to struggle with the text for a while, rather than skim read it. This would help the message remain in the memory.

Activity 2

The *Concise Oxford Dictionary* (1995) offers these as the most common meanings:

language [1] The method of human communication, either spoken or written, consisting of the use of words in an agreed way.

literature [1] written works, esp. those whose value lies in beauty of language or in emotional effect.

It's likely that everyone agreed that language involves the idea of communication, perhaps mentioning that this includes speaking as well as writing. Did anyone include the notion that language is a shared or 'agreed' system used by groups of people?

If everyone agreed that literature refers only to writing, then you have found one difference between the terms. In fact, other senses of the word 'literature' simply refer to anything written down or printed. The primary definition, however, includes the idea of value. Did most people include evaluative words such as 'good'? The dictionary uses the word 'beauty' to refer to the language used in literature. The other idea is the way people react to literature: it affects the emotions.

The key words in summary:

Language	Literature
communication agreed between people spoken or written	written works beauty of language emotional effect

The dictionary definition is not the final word, of course. It simply reflects the way that most people are using the words at a point in history. The definition of literature leaves a number of controversial issues.

The saying 'Beauty is in the eye of the beholder' suggests that it is a personal and subjective decision. People disagree all the time about whether something is beautiful, but the question about whether something is literature or not seems to be decided, regardless of individual opinions about beauty or value. The books of Charles Dickens are definitely considered to be literature; Batman comics might not be counted as literature. The novels of Catherine Cookson are read by far more people than the novels of Dickens. The readers clearly value them, enjoy their emotional effects and consider them to be beautifully written. Yet they are not generally considered to be Literature with a capital L. The capital letter emphasises the special value of the term, just as the distinction between God and a god. The term 'Literature' generally refers to texts that are considered to have special and lasting value by people with influence.

Activity 3

The notion of beauty is the one that is most argued about. Does literature have to be beautiful? What about works that are shocking, even horrifying or ugly? They certainly have an emotional effect. Is this also valuable? Who decides if something is beautiful or not? Often the works that are enjoyed and admired by many people are dismissed as just 'popular' or 'pulp' fiction or verse.

Some works of literature may not have an emotional effect. The German dramatist, Brecht, for example, did not want his plays to draw the audience into a dream world, but wished them to remain alert with the sense that they had a task to accomplish in the real world.

Finally there is the idea of literature as written works. This excludes all spoken culture – poems, songs, stories and plays that are not written down.

Some people have suggested the concept of 'verbal art' to distinguish between language that has been carefully crafted and language that is more spontaneous.

Activity 4

Here is a suggested grouping of the texts in the War anthology according to genres.

Literary	?	Non-literary Verbal art	Spontaneous
Poems Drama / play Prose fiction – novels – short stories	Diary Autobiography	1st-person account (re-written) Magazine article (personal experience) Prose – historical account Newspaper article Obituary	Speech (transcript)

After this preliminary discussion, the answer to whether something is literary or non-literary is not crucial. The important thing is to consider each text on its own merits, responding to its effects and considering the ways in which these are created.

Activity 6

When you listened to someone reading the transcript aloud, it probably did not seem difficult to follow. We are used to hearing pauses, **repetitions, false starts** and **self-corrections** in spoken language.

Repetitions	office where the ... the ... the Chinese steward the other sis ... the other sister
False starts	I would like ... death was preferable at that time
Self-corrections	we were ... we ... we seemed to be cured

These features do not usually occur in written language, so the written representations look strange.

When speaking, we don't have time to choose our words as carefully as in writing. In speech there is more use of vague phrases like:

- this awful pitch

- in perhaps an hour

- sort of thing

- or something.

Activity 7

The extract creates a sense of an elderly, genteel woman. The type of vocabulary Miss Fozzard uses suggests her age and social background. A speaking voice is suggested in the sentence structures.

Type of vocabulary	Example
Colloquial vocabulary	pegging up me stocking, making a bolt for it
Clipped sentence structure	(There was a) Bit of a bombshell today.
Long, loose structure	(the conjunctions – joining words – are printed in bold text.) Apparently, this latest burglary's put the tin hat on things, **and** what with Mrs Sudaby's mother finally going into a home, **and** their TV reception always being so bad, there's not much to keep them in Leeds **so** they're making a bolt for it **and** heading off to Scarborough.
Added comments	apparently added to which
Tense	I'm just pegging ... Mr Sudaby says ... When telling stories, speakers often use the **present tense** to make it sound more immediate, rather than the **past tense** (I was pegging ..., He said) which would often be used when writing a story.

There are no repetitions, self-corrections or indications of pauses.

Activity 8

Here is a version of *The Naval Sister's Tale*, written as an exercise by a student:

> I wouldn't wish seasickness on anyone, no one. My rounds on the ship were every two hours, though normally they would take me an hour to do, tops. Get my hat, run round the ship with hypodermic needle, if anyone's ill, stick it in their bum. Unfortunately, for three days this simple plan failed. The ship had this ghastly pitch and roll, one wave after another, never stopping to rest. Me and the other sister were green with seasickness all night, so our one hour rounds started taking longer and longer. It got to the point where we made it back to the office just in time to leave on the next round. No time to sit, no time to have the drink and sandwiches the Chinese steward would bring us. No rest, just sickness for three days, but we still carried on, and so did the sea. Then after three days, the sickness stopped – just like that. Suddenly I was right as rain, but before that, my God! I'd never felt like that before, or since for that matter. I thought I'd have to resign, just tell them I couldn't take it and to send me home. I was half hoping for a torpedo to end it for me, just 'boom, ploosh, no more waves'. Death or seasickness, I know what I'd choose!

Even though the original words have been radically transformed, the phrasing is still colloquial, capturing the flavour of speech. The colloquial phrases tend to sound modern, except perhaps 'right as rain'. You might think the written version sounds more like someone speaking than her actual words. However, once there is time to plan, the storyteller can structure the narrative, so that the beginning works to intrigue the listener and the ending rounds it off in an effective way.

Activity 10

It is not possible to predict the style and approach used in your own writing of a 3rd-person account. See whether you have used these features of 3rd-person accounts:

- once you were writing about someone as he / she, you may have used a less colloquial style

- you may also have commented as an outside observer on the person's actions and feelings, i.e. made comments that the person themselves would not have been able to

- you may have chosen vocabulary carefully to describe the events and feelings more precisely.

Activity 11

Serge is clearly proud of his painting and Yvan does not want to offend him at all. He mainly repeats the word 'yes'. He is lost for words to comment on the painting: his only question is about the price. Perhaps he feels insecure about his lack of art appreciation, so doesn't want to risk showing his ignorance. Serge talks much more and uses grand terms to talk about the painting: 'similar phase', 'magnetic', 'resonance'. Yvan manages to repeat Serge's comment 'plain' but can't think of a further adjective.

Yvan's repetitions, pauses and unfinished utterances are close to natural speech, as are Serge's clipped sentence structures: '(Do) You like it?'

Despite the fact that their conversation sounds quite natural, the writer's main purpose is to create a dramatic dialogue, not a realistic representation of conversation.

Activity 12

Extract 1 comes close to the amount of interpretation found in books published by Mills & Boon. The characters are described as speaking eagerly, reproachfully, gently; the female kisses, sobs and blushes and the onlookers are respectful and sympathetic. The reader is guided towards a particular reaction to this scene. We must share the attitude and values of the writer.

Extract 2 adds very little comment to the words spoken by the characters, but there is an implied comment in the statements: 'They did not have to answer. They were battle police.'

Activity 13

In Extract 1, George Orwell has conveyed his own emotions of horror, pity and a strange fascination. There is a strong persuasive element in the information he gives. The phrase 'devilish roar of glee' makes the reader share the writer's attitude that it was a barbaric act. However, Orwell's description lingers over the details. The elephant took half an hour to die and Orwell includes gory detail in a sort of close-up: 'the frightful impact of the bullet', 'his mouth slobbered'. The reader is encouraged to feel pity in the choice of vocabulary that emphasises age rather than size and strength: 'shrunken, immensely old', 'sagged flabbily'. The intended audience is probably people who do not live in countries that have problems with violent elephants, as the crowd present at the killing did *not* feel horror, but would be more concerned about the man the elephant had killed.

Extract 2. This editorial is addressed to young, female teenage readers of the magazine, *Bliss*. An equal status of young friends is assumed, although the writer is probably a graduate journalist. This is effective for a magazine that needs to attract its target audience and make them feel part of a young group. The tone is chatty, as if it is a personal letter. There are a large number of colloquial expressions, like 'checked out' and 'on top form' plus slang terms that would be recognised as 'youth' speak, like 'daggy'. The writer has also coined new expressions by compounding or blending existing words: 'depression-free' and 'babelicious' (see further page 76). Existing words are given a deviant spelling to suggest spoken language: 'currazy' 'rockin'' and 'toons'. Depending on your viewpoint, this gives the impression of either lively innovation or sloppy rule-breaking. It is intended for teenage female readers, so the effect is likely to be positive on the intended audience.

Activity 16

The text assumes that:

- only females need help to overcome feelings of insecurity (even though 'it' changes from 'she' to 'we all', the text is clearly targeting females)

- it is common for a girl to 'suffer', feel 'afraid' and that lack of confidence can be 'devastating'

- there is such a thing as the 'right' clothes and make-up

- it is important to leave a room 'correctly' and remove outer garments elegantly

- these skills are important in a career and friendship.

Many male and female readers will resist the implicit values and attitudes of this text.

Activity 17

Here are some examples of nouns you might have noticed in a classroom setting. Each is then tested to see whether it can function as a verb:

(* means it is not used as a verb)

My seat	*I'm going to seat (everybody)*
The floor	*floor (someone with a punch)*
A friend	**friend (someone) but 'befriend'*

Activity 18

Glamorama is a satire on modern materialistic lifestyles, where the most important thing is to have all the status symbols of wealth and fame. There is a latest fashion in everything, so if you want to be in the in-crowd, you have to buy the right brands and labels and make sure they are noticed. Name-dropping is necessary and names are certainly dropped in this passage.

Activity 19

Here is a suggested diagrammatic representation:

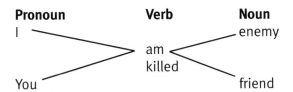

Pronoun **Verb** **Noun**

I

am
killed

enemy

You

friend

If you see a link between 'I' and 'you', 'enemy' and 'friend', you understand not only their related meaning, but their related form. 'I' and 'you' are 1st- and 2nd-person pronouns. A pronoun is a word that can stand in place of a noun, as this line states: 'I am the enemy'; 'you ... my friend'. The verb that occurs between the nouns 'enemy' and 'friend' is 'killed'.

There are various interpretations of this line. Looking at grammatical structure first:

> I am the enemy.
> You killed me.
> You are my friend.
> You killed the enemy.
> You killed your friend.

We could also add: I might *easily* have killed you. I believed you were my enemy, but I realise you are my friend.

But, we should not read a poem simply as grammar. There is a powerful message in this poem against the simplistic division that war makes between people as enemies or friends. Many soldiers in the First World War (and others) felt comradeship with the soldiers in the opposing trenches. Despite the national reasons for war, they had a strong sense that these other men were also ordinary people with lives and families similar to their own.

This analysis and interpretation has used both linguistic terminology and awareness of the historical context. It is an example of how you can 'bridge the gap' between identification of precise grammatical features and your response to and interpretation of the text as a whole.

Activity 20

Most of the adjectives and adverbs could be omitted without altering the basic sentence structure:

> Time stood still as the ribbon of morning sunlight stretched over the scrubland below us.

The resulting text might seem too plain for your taste, or you may have felt that the original was over-written.

Certainly some of the adjectives and adverbs seem redundant – not strictly needed as they add no extra information to the text: 'blurry haze', 'oppressive and overbearing', 'lolling idly'. You may feel that such repetition is elegant or irritating.

Activity 22

heavy – light
that's such a drag, it's weighing me down, carrying a lot of baggage around, lighten up, walking on air, floating

inside – outside
the in-crowd, in the know, the centre of attention, an outsider, on the outside looking in, far out

hard – soft
that's tough, thick-skinned, stiff, uptight, a hard life, don't be so soft, go all mushy, melting, hang loose

dark – light
never darken my door, light of my life, gleam of hope

cold – hot
that leaves me cold, freeze someone out, chill out, hot blooded, warm welcome

Activity 23

These images are used:

> split up, sever, links, brave move, make a clean break, break up, let him go, major step
> dumping, let down, fallen
> drag on, tick over, fizzle out

There are images of a relationship tying two people together. This can have positive connotations in words such as 'link' and 'bond'. Images of breaking free sound painful: 'sever', 'split up'. It is interesting that we say people 'fall', rather than 'rise' in love. When one person moves away, the other feels 'let down' or 'dumped'. A phrase often used on confessional shows like Jerry Springer's is 'I love him / her to bits', before the expletives and fists start flying – it certainly *is* a destructive image. The notion of appetite has been used for centuries and modern terms like 'tasty' retain this idea. Passion is often described as fire, as in related images like 'fizzle out'.

Activity 28 on semantic field returns to this concept of related images.

Activity 26

These are some phrases that include the word 'common'. The first few have negative connotations for nearly everyone, but the phrase 'the common people' can have different connotations for different people. The Pulp song of that name used the phrase in an ambiguous way. This word has a range of connotations, positive as well as negative. One of its meanings is 'shared by many people', but this can be a positive or negative quality depending on your outlook. Derived words such as 'commune' and 'communal' have positive connotations, whereas 'communist' is often used with negative connotations.

> common or garden, common as muck, commonplace, out of the common, the common people, the common cold, by common consent, common-law wife, common room, common property, common knowledge, to have something in common, common sense

Activity 27

The adjectives used are:

> vulgar, dirty, ugly, unpleasant, false

There is also the phrase 'wallowing in litter'. There are several words related to the semantic of field of dirt. Certainly these words have negative connotations. The verb 'wallow' is often collocated with animals. It is not accurate for the speaker to say 'there is no other word for it', as there are other words that denote the action – swimming or splashing around in. His particular choice conveyed his disgust, because the word is often collocated with pigs, and pigs, in turn, are associated with dirt.

The speaker also chooses the word vulgar. Its earliest known source is the Latin word 'vulgaris' which meant 'common people' as opposed to the 'nobles' / elite classes in Roman society. So, in that sense, Blackpool is vulgar, because a number of ordinary people explained on the same radio programme why they enjoy holidays in Blackpool. But the speaker meant more than that when he chose the word 'vulgar'. He was not simply describing the groups of people holidaying there. He intended to convey his own opinion about their value. The connotations of the word 'vulgar' are negative.

Activity 28

The full text is from a newspaper article:

BBC bosses' orders to cut shots of snooker players smoking made 'an absolute nonsense' of coverage of the Embassy World Snooker Championships at the Crucible, it is being claimed. The pro-smoking group, FOREST, has launched an all-out attack on the BBC policy.

It quotes top sports writer Ian Wooldridge as saying television screens were full of 'Headless torsos, disembodied legs and unidentified buttocks.'

The no-smoking instruction followed an initiative by BBC managing director Bill Cotton to cut down the number of shots of snooker players smoking. Mr Cotton has been under a great deal of pressure from the anti-smoking lobby. But a BBC spokesman denied that coverage of the championships had been affected or spoilt in any way at all. 'Sport is in a nutcracker here – it is in the middle of a very difficult situation.'

The situation is described in terms from a siege or shoot-out.

Activity 29

Questions. Some are requests for information: 'can you put it anywhere'. The stallholder asks for personal information, but probably just to make polite conversation. Others function as invitations. These are often abbreviated forms, such as '(are) you having a go boys'.

Commands. The structures such as 'see what you can nick' have a similar function of encouraging the boys to try their luck. Other imperatives are used to instruct, such as 'chalk your thingy mate'.

Exclamations. There are none.

Echoes. The stallholder often echoes the boys, as a way of showing that he is listening and interested.

> No we've been playing a football tournament.
> You've been playing football.

Activity 30

Most of the sentences are complex. Some have embedded clauses (shown in italics):

> Everyone, *including those who say that they never dream*, probably dreams during REM sleep.

There are a few examples of simple sentences with only one verb (shown in italics):

> Only one thing *is* certain.
> Sleep *is* necessary.
> Sleep deprivation *is* an effective technique of brainwashing.

There is only one example of a compound sentence:

> The effect is like drunkenness, *but* the person can pull himself together *and* behave normally for short periods.

There is one minor sentence that begins with a conjunction (shown in italics):

> *But* a dream is only remembered if one wakes almost at once.

This extract is from an essay which tends to use complex sentences with an occasional simple statement.

Activity 31

The opening sentence to this chapter is strikingly long. There are many clauses co-ordinated by 'and' up to the phrase 'I'm taking it all in blankly', when the structures become complex. The effect is of someone taking in one thing after another, hence the term 'periodic' sentence. The scene appears chaotic and confused. The style seems rather loose and rambling, which resembles the perspective of the main character.

Activity 32

Most people find it hard to remember stretches of language word for word, unless the language has patterns of repeated sounds. In a culture that can record the language in permanent form – writing or tapes – it is not important to be able to remember accurately. But perhaps oral societies used this memorability factor in poems, songs, stories and prayers, in order to pass them on to the next generation. If language is patterned, it stays in the mind. In the case of poems and songs, this may be a delight; in the case of adverts, it can be irritating. Even if their aims and effects are quite different, poetry and advertising share similar devices. The novelist and poet Salman Rushdie gained less fame, but more money for his advertising slogan for fresh cream: 'Naughty but nice'.

Activity 33

The choices shape the meaning in slightly different ways. The change from 'Dead' to 'Doomed' introduces a longer vowel sound, which resonates longer, possibly similar to the ringing of a bell? Although the word 'doom' can mean 'death', it has the wider meaning of grim fate or destiny. The young people are not only dead, but fated to die. We might ask why this was their destiny. Playing an anthem *for* someone adds a note of homage to the notion of playing an anthem *to* them. These two words are **prepositions**.

The change from 'minute-' to 'passing-' bells makes the idea of brevity clearer. Readers might puzzle over the meaning of 'minute-bells'. The first choice of referring to the young men in a distant way as 'these' was rejected in favour of the more personal 'you', but then finally chosen in preference to 'you'. This was obviously a more tricky decision. The use of 'you' makes the poem sound as if it addressed to the soldiers, but they are not present. The choice becomes more precise in each draft.

The emphasis is taken off the speed of death to the sheer numbers suggested by 'herds'. This word also suggests that the soldiers have no more value than animals, killed to serve their masters. The final choice of 'cattle' keeps all these associations, but gives a more precise image of a particular animal. The poet might have preferred 'herds' for its meaning, but the sound of 'cattle' will be taken up in the next lines for an onomatopoeic effect.

The change from 'solemn' to 'monstrous' conveys anger and disgust, rather than a respectful sadness. The respectful mood only appears in the funeral *scenes* (final stanza), not the dying (first stanza). The change of determiner (our, more, the) may seem trivial, particularly as the final choice was for the most neutral. Perhaps the poet decided it wasn't important whether the guns were yours, ours or theirs.

In the first draft, Owen personifies the guns in a shocking cartoon-like image. We can imagine the barrels of the guns open like a mouth jeering, but can mouths be blind? Perhaps this was an over-clever mixture of images. (The term 'mixed metaphor' describes this type of clash of images. There are obvious examples in everyday speech, for example 'Every time she opens her mouth, she puts her foot in it.') The poet keeps the image of mouths, but emphasises the sounds emerging from them in the phrase 'stuttering rifles'. Although images are often visual, they can appeal to the other four senses, in this case hearing. The final draft provides a vivid auditory image – the jerky sound suggested by 'stuttering' is enforced by 'rattle', which is often collocated with death, as in 'death rattle'. The sound of the words emphasises this meaning with the repeated plosive 't' sounds. The long vowel sound in 'words' doesn't work as well as the short vowel sounds in 'rapid'. Although we might feel that a similar idea has been unnecessarily repeated in the three words, 'stutter, rattle, rapid', their sound qualities make them an effective choice.

Activity 34

Here is a breakdown of each question, that you could use as the basis for planning notes for your answer.

1	**Examine**	**(ways)**	**Refer**
	'Inspection'	ideas	ways language varies
	'Strange Meeting'	feelings	
	'Poem of choice'	attitudes	
	values		
	author's purposes		

2	**Compare**	**Examine**	**Refer**
	The Naval Sister's Tale	ways writers tell stories	form
	'The Obituary of Captain Goodwin'		style
	'Text of choice'		vocabulary

Before writing your answer, you should note the key points you wish to make about the aspects in the middle column. Then note the features of language that are relevant. The second question points out that you should refer not only to vocabulary, but also to form and style. To gain marks in the higher bands, it is important to be able to comment on these broader aspects of overall structure and approach, so make sure you include them in the first question as well.

This module counts for 35% of the AS qualification, or 17.5% of the total A Level marks.

ASSESSMENT OBJECTIVES

The skills and knowledge that you develop in this module, and that will be assessed in your coursework, are defined by the examination board's Assessment Objectives. These require that you:

1 communicate clearly the knowledge, understanding and insights gained from the combination of literary and linguistic study, using appropriate terminology and accurate written expression (5% of the final AS mark; 2.5% of the final A Level mark)

2 distinguish, describe and interpret variation in meaning and form in responding to literary and non-literary texts (10% of the final AS mark; 5% of the final A Level mark)

3 respond to and analyse texts, using literary and linguistic concepts and approaches (10% of the final AS mark; 5% of the final A Level mark)

4 show understanding of the ways contextual variation and choices of form, style and vocabulary shape the meanings of texts (5% of the final AS mark; 2.5% of the final A Level mark)

5 identify and consider the ways attitudes and values are created and conveyed in speech and writing (5% of the final AS mark; 2.5% of the final A Level mark).

Development from Module 1

Module 1 and Module 2 both use set texts as the focus. However, there are differences **a)** in the type of texts, and **b)** in the issues to be studied.

Module 1	Module 2
Open book	Closed book
Set anthology of short texts	Choice of two longer, complete texts
Both literary and non-literary genres	Literary genres
Genre focus on poetry	Genre focus on prose
Two questions	One question
Focus on devices of poetry	Focus on devices of prose
Comparison of different genres and contexts	Focus on language change

The exam question for Module 2 will ask you to compare and contrast extracts from each text. The starting point for *comparison* is that each pair of texts has similar themes and, possibly, genres.

The starting point for *contrast* is the different context in which each text was produced. One important difference is the era in which each was written. There is a gap of at least one hundred years, so there will be evidence of language change over time.

Language also changes from one cultural context to another, so, for example, you should be aware of variation in language use in the American texts.

You should also consider similarities and differences in the purpose and audience for each text, and discuss the ways each extract reveals attitudes and values conveyed in the texts as a whole.

So, whichever pair of texts you choose for study, you should consider these questions:

- What type (sub-genre) of prose text is it?

- How is this type of text structured?

- What is the historical and social context of the text?

- What changes in language are apparent in the text?

- How does the language vary depending on the purpose and audience?

- How are ideas, themes and characters presented?

- What attitudes and values does the text express?

You may feel more confident about discussing themes, meaning, attitudes and values, i.e. understanding *what* the text is expressing. However, the Assessment Objectives also require discussion of *how* such meanings are conveyed. Words in the Assessment Objectives such as 'analyse', 'ways' and 'form' all indicate the need to explain how the text works:

- Objective 1 specifies the use of appropriate *terminology*.

- Objective 2 asks you to make connections between the meaning and the *form*.

- Objective 3 requires you to respond to and *analyse* texts, using literary and linguistic concepts and approaches.

- Objective 4 refers to the *ways* that meanings are shaped.

- Objective 5 refers to the *ways* that attitudes and values are created.

This book does not provide interpretation of an individual text's meaning, themes, attitudes and values. It can, however, provide a repertoire of useful approaches, concepts and terminology. The activities ask you to apply these concepts in close reading and analysis of example texts. These skills can then be transferred to the study of your chosen books.

What concepts are needed?

Linguistic concepts

An essential linguistic concept is that of *language change*. You need to have an understanding of the broad principles:

- Why does language change?

- In what ways does it change?

- How has language changed over the past one hundred or more years?

- How does language change according to cultural context?

As in Module 1, you should refer to the systematic linguistic framework described on page 2.

Discourse
changes in the
structure /organisation
of texts and genres

Semantics
changes in
the ways in which
meanings are
communicated

Pragmatics
changes in the ways
implied meanings are
conveyed in social
practice

Phonology
changes in
the sounds of
the language

Graphology
changes in
conventions
for spelling,
punctuation, layout

Morphology
changes in
word formation

Lexis
changes in
vocabulary

Grammar
changes
in word
order and
sentence
structure

A systematic framework for language analysis

This hierarchical framework provides a repertoire from which you can select relevant aspects. Not all of these will be significant for a particular text. It may not be possible, for example, to detect changes in pronunciation from a written text. Modern editions of texts may change the original typeface and layout, so that it is not possible to comment on the original aspects of graphology, apart from punctuation.

This module will build on the terms and concepts already introduced in Module 1 for the description of vocabulary and grammar, so you should add to your personal glossary of terms.

Literary concepts

Important literary concepts for this study of prose texts are the *narrative devices* used by writers to create character and viewpoint. These in turn help to convey attitudes and values:

- **narrative voice**

- **point of view**

- **representation of speech** and thought.

Organising your study of the two texts

This module begins with an exploration of the concept of language change and moves on to the analysis of narrative devices. Examples are taken from a range of sources, but the skills and concepts can be applied to the two texts you have chosen. If you are reading the texts for the first time as you work through this module, you should read the book from the earlier period first, so that you can examine features of language that have changed. It would be useful to begin the modern book simultaneously, so that you can make comparisons. Once you have read both texts, you will be able to analyse the narrative devices of each. Keep a record of aspects of both language change and narrative devices in the texts, as you work through the activities.

Language change

This module is called 'The Changing Language of Literature'. The pairs of texts are separated by at least one hundred years, so changes over time will be an important focus. This type of variation over time is called **diachronic variation**, but it is important to be aware of other aspects of **synchronic variation** at any one point in time. In the year 2001, for example, there are differences in the form of English used in different regions and countries, in different social groups, and by individuals depending on the situation they are in.

Types of language change

Idiolect
an individual's distinctive style

Register
appropriate style for the situation

Geographical dialect
evidence of the regional origin

Social dialect
features common to a social group

Temporal dialect
features distinctive of a time in history

A text can be located at any point between these axes.

Temporal dialect

Changes in the English language are obvious if you look at texts like these:

Beowulf (around 750–800)

Hwæt! We Gardena in geardagum,
peodcyninga, prym gefrunon,
hu ða æpelingas ellen fremedon.

The Canterbury Tales, by Chaucer (1343–1400)

Whan that aprille with his shoures soote
The droghte of march hath perced to the roote,
and bathed every veyne in swich licour
Of which vertu engendred is the flour;

Macbeth, by Shakespeare (1564–1616)

LADY MACBETH: That which hath made them drunk hath made me bold;
What hath quenched them hath given me fire. Hark! Peace!
It was the owl that shrieked, the fatal bellman,
Which gives the stern'st good-night. He is about it.
The doors are open; and the surfeited grooms
Do mock their charge with snores. I have drugged their possets,
That death and nature do contend about them,
Whether they live or die.

In the case of *Beowulf* and *The Canterbury Tales*, it is like reading another language and most people use a translation into Modern English.

Archaic language

The terms **archaic** and **archaism** refer to language features that are no longer in current use, for example 'forthwith' and 'aforesaid'. Because they are still found in situations that are ceremonial and conservative such as in religious services and legal documents, it is difficult to distinguish archaic words from ones which are simply rare or formal. A good dictionary will indicate in brackets if the word is archaic, dialect, poetic, colloquial, slang or obsolete.

Some grammatical structures are no longer in current use, so may be termed archaic. The verb endings '-eth' are no longer used in Modern English, without drawing attention to themselves, for example 'The axe man cometh.'

Although there are modern translations of Thomas More's *Utopia* from the Latin original, the set text is a translation produced by Ralph Robinson in 1551. Utopia is an imaginary state described in More's political satire and the word 'utopia' is now used without a capital letter to refer to any real or imaginary place believed to be ideal. The word 'dystopia' was formed to describe the opposite – a place where everything is as bad as possible.

| **ACTIVITY 1** | **C3.2** |

Read the following extract from *Utopia*, by Thomas More.

- Identify features of grammar and vocabulary that seem unfamiliar.

- Check the vocabulary in a dictionary to see whether it is archaic.

- Compare each grammatical structure with a modern equivalent. Discuss whether it is simply a formal style or no longer in current use.

Now read the commentary on pages 102–103.

Again, in some parts of the land these serving-men (for so be these damned persons called) do no common work, but as every private man needeth labourers, so he cometh into the market place and there hireth some of them for meat and drink and a certain limited wages by the day, somewhat cheaper than he should hire a free man. It is also lawful for them to chastise the sloth of these serving-men with stripes. By this means they never lack work, and besides the gaining of their meat and drink, every one of them be apparelled in one colour. Their heads be not polled or shaven, but rounded a little above the ears, and the tip of the one ear is cut off. Every one of them may take meat and drink of their friends, and also a coat of their own colour, but to receive money is death, as well to the giver as to the receiver. And no less jeopardy it is for a free man to receive money of a serving-man for any manner of cause, and likewise for serving-men to touch weapons.

Dated language

Activity 2 asks you to identify features that appear **old-fashioned** or **dated** (no longer in common usage) to you. These may not strictly be archaisms, but formal or less common usage.

Texts written a hundred or so years ago do not display such obvious differences and may use language in a way that seems remarkably similar to the way language is used today. However, you should still be able to identify aspects of language change.

ACTIVITY 2	C3.2

Read the two diary extracts.

- Can you estimate the century / year when each was written?
- Which do you think is the more recent text?
- Identify features that seem old-fashioned to you.

Now read the commentary on pages 103–104.

EXTRACT 1

I wrote to Mrs Clarkson and Luff – went with Ellen to Rydale. Coleridge came in with a sack-full of Books etc, and a Branch of mountain ash. He had been attacked by a cow. He came over by Grisdale. A furious wind. Mr Simpson drank tea. William very poorly – we went to bed lateish. I slept in sittingroom.

EXTRACT 2

Went to park. Full of girls who sit up, bending over their male companions who are lying down receiving their kissings & caressings. It is disgusting to watch. No wonder Billy Graham thought our parks so foul. But I'm sure Hyde is the worst. There is so much riff-raff living near.

Idiolect

Any speaker (or writer) has an idiolect – a style which is like a fingerprint in identifying them. Forensic linguistics is now accepted as evidence in court cases, where there is doubt about the identity of a recorded voice or a written text. Derek Bentley (hanged in 1953) finally received a pardon when it was shown that his 'statements' to the police included language that was not his. Bentley was almost illiterate and could not have used the sophisticated constructions that were written in 'his' statements. One construction that was often used was, 'I *then* went to Craig's house.' Statistical evidence shows that this structure is only used in writing – very commonly in police reports; speakers always say, '*Then* I went'.

Literary authorship studies try to identify the writer of works, for example whether the play *Edward III* was, or was not, written by Shakespeare.

'Plagiarism' refers to the copying of another person's writing without acknowledgement. This can also be reliably identified by computer programs that analyse style.

Each person's individual style is influenced by the other variables – the time at which they live, their age (and possibly gender), their social and regional background, and the situation in which they are writing or speaking.

ACTIVITY 3   C3.1A

Read the following extract from a letter to the *Daily Telegraph*.

- In what year do you think this was published?

- Assess the origins of the writer – age, gender, social and regional background.

- In groups, compare the extract in a pyramiding exercise. Try to reach an agreement at each stage. Make reference to evidence in the text.

Now read the commentary on page 104.

> Several years ago, while conducting researches in the Bodleian Library, I had occasion to use its lavatory. Above the paper dispenser, someone had written in an impeccable hand: 'Sociology degrees – help yourself.'
>
> The author of this lapidary dictum had preserved his anonymity, but my suspicion lies with a certain regius professor.

Register

Register refers to the subtle variations people make to their use of language depending on the situation they find themselves in. The situation can vary according to:

- mode (whether speaking or writing)

- purpose (what you are trying to achieve)

- audience (whom you are addressing)

- topic (what you are talking or writing about).

Register can be thought of as a scale ranging from the most **formal** use, for example the ceremonial language of weddings and funerals, with a public audience and a solemn purpose, to the most **informal** use, for example in casual conversations between friends. The stretches in between are susceptible to change. Letters to broadsheet newspapers, as in the example in Activity 3, have a public audience, so are often written in a careful, detached style, but you can see more colloquial letters to newspapers today. The deliberate choice of an unconventional register can suggest that the speaker / writer is relaxed, confident, unconventional. Politicians in the House of Commons keep to some established phrases, for example 'My honourable friend', but the use of more informal language gets them noticed by the media.

| ACTIVITY 4 | C3.1A |

Read the following extract, which was awarded First Prize in a competition.

- Assess the register of the text.

- What do you think this prize was awarded for?

- Explain your decision.

Now read the commentary on pages 104–105.

FIRST PRIZE

The move from a structuralist account in which capital is understood to structure social relations in relatively homologous ways to a view of hegemony in which power relations are subject to repetition, convergence, and rearticulation brought the question of temporality into the thinking of structure, and marked a shift from a form of Althusserian theory that takes structural totalities as theoretical objects to one in which the insights into the contingent possibility of structure inaugurate a renewed conception of hegemony as bound up with the contingent sites and strategies of the rearticulation of power.

Geographical dialect

It is sometimes possible to identify the area a speaker comes from by their pronunciation, vocabulary and grammar. In the 1950s, the broadcaster, Wilfred Pickles, wrote a version of Bible stories to convey features of the Yorkshire dialect that was associated with his name. The story of 'The Prodigal Son', for example, contained these phrases:

> Ah 'ope ther's none of yer stuck-up enough ... when 'e were wahming 'is 'ands bi t' fire.

Vocabulary like 'stuck-up' is colloquial, rather than typical of a particular region. There is some grammatical variation in 'he were' rather than 'he was', but most of the changes are to the spelling, indicating an accent. It is pronunciation differences that identify regional varieties, more than grammar and vocabulary these days.

Activity 5 explores the use of spelling changes to indicate regional accents. Notice whether the texts you are studying attempt to represent pronunciation by non-standard spelling. This may be done for some of the characters, while the representation of other characters' speech is not marked in this way. Does this suggest that their pronunciation is 'normal'?

ACTIVITY 5 | C3.1A | C3.3

In groups, each write a few lines in various dialects or strong accents that you are familiar with. (For variety, think of characters from film and TV.)

Pass these to another group to read out loud.

Discuss these questions:

1 Why are written versions of geographical dialect and accent so often associated with the comic and stereotypical?

2 How far can / could the spelling be changed?

3 Do the markers of geographical origins also provide indications of the social class of the speaker?

Now read the commentary on page 105.

Standard English

The term **Standard English (SE)** refers to the dialect previously spoken in the areas around London, Oxford and Cambridge. It is now the form accepted as the model for educated written usage in the UK and is used as the basis of grammars for foreign learners of English. As it has this prestige, it is used by people regardless of region. The standard form of pronunciation is called **Received Pronunciation (RP)** but many people retain their regional accent and attitudes towards other accents are changing slowly, as they are given more prominence in the media, for example. (See Activity 12.)

The texts you are studying may have characters whose speech has features of a regional dialect, whether this is a region in Britain or other English-speaking countries such as the United States.

ACTIVITY 6 | C3.2

Occasionally a novel is entirely narrated in a regional variety of English. The following is an extract from *Lifting the Latch*, by Sheila Stewart. The writer spent two years recording the memoirs of an Oxfordshire man, born in 1902, which she then put into written form as a piece of social history. Although she will have edited his actual words, she has retained features of his accent and dialect.

Read the extract.

• Pick out the features of regional dialect (vocabulary and grammar) and accent.

• Identify the corresponding standard forms.

Now read the commentary on pages 105–106.

Mary were a topping piano player; any snatch of tune thee sang to her, any torn sheet of music thee set before her, her 'ud pick up the remnant, full-chord and tack on the twiddly bits. Her must have spent a fortune on sheet-music. Any new song that come out her sought after it.

- Choose and analyse a short extract of a character's regional dialect from one of your set texts.

Social dialect

There is an overlap between a geographical and a social dialect. Because SE and RP tend to be used by middle-class speakers, regional dialects are associated with membership of lower classes.

In *The Adventures of Huckleberry Finn*, Mark Twain includes two interesting notes to preface the book. The first is tongue-in-cheek, claiming not to have any motive or moral in mind. The second explains the use of dialects in the text. He says that there are three distinct dialects and four modified varieties of the ordinary 'Pike-Country' dialect.

Most readers are aware of only three voices in the story: Huck's dialect, the more refined speech of the adult carers and Jim's Black English dialect. Their regional origins are the same, but their social backgrounds differ. The fictional character, Huck Finn, is the narrator. His recognisable style (idiolect) combines features of his geographical, social and temporal origins. It differs from his friend, Jim's, speech.

A C T I V I T Y 7	**C3.2**

Read the following extracts from *The Adventures of Huckleberry Finn*, by Mark Twain. (You may also answer these questions about the 1st-person narrator or speaking character in your own text.)

- What region does the speaker come from?

- When did s/he live?

- How old is s/he?

- What is her/his social and educational background?

- Identify the significant language features.

Now read the commentary on page 106.

EXTRACT 1

The widow she cried over me, and called me a poor lost lamb, and she called me a lot of other names, too, but she never meant no harm by it. She put me in them new clothes again, and I couldn't do nothing but sweat and sweat, and feel all cramped up. Well, then, the old thing commenced again. The widow rung a bell for supper, and you had to come to time. When you got to the table you couldn't go right to eating, but you had to wait for the widow to tuck down her head and grumble a little over the victuals, though there warn't really anything the matter with them.

EXTRACT 2

'Goodness gracious, is dat you, Huck? En you ain' dead – you ain' drownded – you is back agin? It's too good for true, honey, it's too good for true. Lemme look at you chile, lemme feel o' you. No, you ain' dead! You's back agin, 'live en soun', jis de same ole Huck – de same ole Huck, thanks to goodness!'

Fictional dialect

Some fictional characters do not belong to an existing temporal, geographical or social group. If the setting for a novel is in the future or an imaginary world, then the writer must select an existing 'dialect' or invent one for the characters. This is also the case for non-human characters, such as animals or monsters. Notice whether the writer chooses the standard dialect of the time, which may seem neutral, or a variation of the standard. Activity 8 looks at the choice of a **non-standard** form of speech for a character and asks you to assess how the effect of this dialect on the character is constructed.

ACTIVITY 8   C3.2

The following phrases are taken from the *The BFG* by Roald Dahl, and are the first words spoken by the giant. For this activity, concentrate on the grammatical forms, rather than the vocabulary. Activity 14 will examine the formation of words in more detail.

- Identify the non-standard grammar – verb forms and pronouns.

- Is it consistent?

- Are these features of a particular regional dialect?

- Why has the writer chosen to make the Giant speak like this?

- Is it significant that the girl character uses SE?

Now read the commentary on pages 106–107.

'I is hungry!' the Giant boomed. [...]

The Giant let out a bellow of laughter. 'Just because I is a giant, you think I is a man-gobbling cannybull!' he shouted. 'You is about right! Giants is all cannybully and murderful! And they *does* gobble up human beans! We is in Giant Country now! Giants is everywhere around! Out there us has the famous Bonecrunching Giant! Bonecrunching Giant crunches up two wopsey whiffling human beans for supper every night! Noise is earbursting! Noise of crunching bones goes crackety-crack for miles around!'

[...]

'Bonecrunching Giant only gobbles human beans from Turkey,' the Giant said. 'Every night Bonecruncher is galloping off to Turkey to gobble Turks.'

[...]

'Bonecrunching Giant says Turks is tasting oh ever so much juicier and more scrumdiddlyumptious! Bonecruncher says Turkish human beans has a glamourly flavour. He says Turks from Turkey is tasting of turkey.'

[...]

'Of course they would!' the Giant shouted. 'Every human bean is diddly and different. Some is scrumdiddlyumptious and some is uckyslush. Greeks is all full of uckyslush. No giant is eating Greeks, ever.'

[...]

'Greeks from Greece is all tasting greasy,' the Giant said.

Assessing the influences

As the previous activities have shown, historical period is only one of several influences on the form of language. Language changes according to the geographical and social context as well. It is important not to think of English having *one* consistent style at each period in time.

ACTIVITY 9   C3.1A

Read the following three texts.

- Estimate the date each was written. Justify your decision.

- Suggest a context for each – where might it be printed?

- Find points of comparison and contrast between the texts on scales such as:

  - standard v. non-standard
  - archaic v. modern
  - formal v. informal.

- Refer to choice of vocabulary and sentence structure

Now read the commentary on pages 107–108.

EXTRACT 1 (Sunrise)

On a beautiful evening in June, along with a number of companions, I walked forth in a locality where the skyline was sufficiently well-marked to allow of our having a good view of the setting sun. We noted the objects which rendered his resting place the more easily definable, as we had resolved to return to the same spot the next morning, in order to behold the sun rise.

With an effort, we managed to rise at the untimely hour of four o'clock, and a little later we arrived at the selected spot. Looking in the opposite direction we observed the approach of the Spirit of Light, preceded by the fiery arrows which he sent out before him. As the mantle of cloudy drapery slowly unfolded itself, we noticed that it was covered by a network of dew, which sparkled in a variety of brilliant colours.

EXTRACT 2 (Chitra's last journey)

Fried crab was one of the side dishes served and Chitra and I ventured to try it, but Raj doubted that the operation would be a success with a dry remark to the effect that we were the 'soft-soaped generation' that did not want to get its fingers soiled at table. He was right; I decided to abandon the exercise and Chitra pushed her plate away saying perhaps it wasn't the best thing to eat crab in such an interior part of the country.

She had some difficulty with the cane dining chair so Raj got a cushion for her which solved the situation.

Hunger sharpened by a little of the glass that cheers – Chitra did not share the glass – we set to and enjoyed the fare including the dessert of watalappan, deliciously made.

EXTRACT 3 ('Doin' me bit to prove we're still on top)

Personally I has not seen much of them Olympics. What with all the meticulous preparation required by your modern professional, for Darren Tackle there is not enough hours in the day what can afford to be wasted watching one long parade of posh sports.

But old Demo, our coach, has gone Olympic batty, bringing in rowing machines to the gym, running videos of some geezer in a dinghy to show us how to do a man-marking job on free-flowing Brazilians, telling Wattsy to go all patriotic and get hisself an Audley Harrison barnet job.

Why does language change?

Language change is inevitable – nothing stands still. There are many possible causes, but like the case of someone oversleeping, there is likely to be a combination of causes, rather than one clear cause.

The following activities look at some theories about the possible causes of language change:

- ease
- fashion
- regularity
- contact with others
- mistakes
- need.

Ease

Ease of articulation seems to be the cause of some changes in pronunciation. Look at Activity 10 and the three lists of words.

ACTIVITY 10 | **WO3.1** **WO3.2** **WO3.3**

Work in pairs.

- One of you should say the words in the three lists. Try to speak naturally, rather than reading each one aloud carefully.

- The other of you should turn to the commentary and listen carefully while the other says the words aloud.

- Tell your partner what you heard.

- Say each of the words again to check how you pronounce them.

Now read the commentary on page 108.

List 1	List 2	List 3
postcard	hamster	every
football	Neil	factory
hot water bottle	Gail	nursery
singing a song	drawing	family
fasten	Sue and me	chocolate
castle	India and Pakistan	
often		
handkerchief		

Regularity

The impulse to make the language regular seems to lie behind other changes. Some irregular verbs are in a state of change towards regular '-ed' endings. Which of the following do you use?

dream → dreamt or dreamed
dive → dove or dived
speed → sped or speeded

Other irregular verbs became regular many years ago:

shave → shove → shaved

'I've gotten it' is often disliked as an Americanism, but 'gotten' was the common usage in British English; it still exists in phrases like 'ill-gotten gains' and fits the pattern of other verbs:

get   got   gotten
eat   ate   eaten
write wrote written

Mistakes

The word 'pease' was the singular form, but people mistakenly thought the 's' ending was a plural and so the word 'pea' emerged.

Some people have suggested the role of children in language change: 'No one has ever yet been able to prevent what passes from mouth to ear from getting altered on the way.' (William Whitney, quoted in Aitchison, *Language, Progress or Decay*, 1991) But others think it is unlikely that children have enough influence to persuade people to imitate them. However, it is not only children who have to cope with an everyday version of Chinese Whispers, where the sounds may be indistinct and the hearer makes their best guess. The dangerous snake used to be called 'a nadder', but this was heard as 'an adder'. This is now the standard form. The Giant in *The BFG*, by Roald Dahl pronounces the word 'cannibal' as 'cannybull', perhaps mistakenly connecting the word with the animal 'bull'.

ACTIVITY 11   WO3.1

Can you explain the causes of the following changes:

1 hisself

2 theirselves

3 he might of gone

4 she seen it

5 an apron (originally napron)

6 brothers (originally brethren)

7 bone → bonfire (change in pronunciation of the vowel sound)

8 break → breakfast (change in pronunciation of the vowel sound)

9 child → children (change in pronunciation of the vowel sound)

10 know → knowledge (change in pronunciation of the vowel sound)

Now read the commentary on pages 108–109.

The first three suggested causes were connected with the internal workings of a language becoming gradually easier and more consistent. Other theories are to do with external pressures from the social context in which language is used. Activities 10, 11 and 12 provide a very brief introduction to some of the issues. There is not scope in a book like this to do justice to such a complex area. So, for example, there is no discussion of political influences and pressures on the language. Military conquest and occupation are causes of language change that can be seen in the history of English. Roman, Viking and French invasions all changed the language spoken in the United Kingdom. On the other hand, the English language has 'invaded' other countries.

Fashion

Sometimes language changes because of fashion: people simply enjoy something new. Different forms of language may be adapted because they are seen as more attractive, similar to trends in clothing fashion. Styles of clothing change, not because there is a need to wear shorter or longer hemlines, but because people enjoy variety. Once a style or colour is seen as fashionable a lot of people start wearing something similar. The reverse is also true – shellsuits became suddenly non-fashionable. In language, there are noticeable, frequent changes in the words used to express approval or disapproval. In the year 2000, for example, the author noted the use of 'pants' and 'mingin' by students to express negative attitudes, but these may have fallen out of use by the time you read this book. Activity 12 asks you to collect current terms.

Contact with others

When people are in contact with others that they like, they tend to behave like them. In the same way, they will take care not to let their behaviour resemble that of people they do not like. This is the concept of **convergence** and **divergence**, which can be observed in language. Some English people return from a holiday in the United States with strong traces of American English; others live there for years without any noticeable influence. Nowadays, the possibility for contact with speakers of other varieties of English is great and people tend to pick up language habits from each other – or decide not to, if they want to distance themselves from that group. American terms and spelling conventions have entered contemporary British English usage, because of the influence, for example, of the media and computer technology.

Need

As society changes, language has to adapt to cope. The need for new vocabulary is most obvious to name new things, such as modern technology, or to rename concepts in different ways, as in new job titles, such as Human Resources instead of Personnel. Changing social attitudes and practices are reflected in awareness of the power of language to stereotype groups, often in derogatory ways. The term 'political correctness' has acquired some negative connotations, because of the way it is used dismissively by those who are comfortable with the status quo, but there have been a number of positive changes.

ACTIVITY 12

In groups, collect examples of language change that could be attributed to each of the three social causes mentioned above: fashion, contact with others and need. Try also to find examples of language change that could be attributed to politics.

Consider pronunciation and vocabulary. Try to find examples of grammatical changes.

Suggested areas:

• different terms for words, for example 'good' and 'bad'

• the influence of other accents, for example in the media

• words for new development, for example in technology

• new names for existing products, for example trousers

• the influence of 'political correctness'.

Now read the commentary on page 109.

How do people respond to language change?

Although language change is inevitable, the process is slow and uneven. While some people enjoy anything new and different, there is an equally strong resistance to change from other groups. You can see an impulse towards change in youth culture and the media, but a strong tendency towards language preservation in legal and official contexts.

Conservative elements of society tend to react to change with hostility. It is seen as a general deterioration, like an old car getting rusty. Of course, it is only recent changes that cause distress; new varieties of language take time to be accepted and are first termed slang, non-standard, Americanisms, or simply incorrect. Some changes do not take hold, but others become accepted as standard. No one complains about changes that happened long before they were born, but it is interesting to realise that most changes met with some resistance at the time.

One change in pronunciation was the abbreviation of the past tense ending '-ed'. At the time the change was happening, it was criticised. Jonathan Swift wrote in *A Proposal for Correcting, Improving and Ascertaining the English Tongue*:

What does your lordship think of the words 'drudg'd,' 'disturb'd,' 'rebuk'd,' 'fledg'd,' and a thousand others everywhere to be met with in prose as well as verse? Where, by leaving out a vowel to save a syllable, we form so jarring a sound, and so difficult to utter, that I have often wondered how it could ever obtain.

Nowadays these are the standard pronunciations.

Younger people tend to enjoy new ways of using language. But they might feel some hostility to language that seems old-fashioned. Language from earlier periods can leave an impression of over-formality, but it cannot be that people living in past centuries were all dull and conventional. Perhaps it is because we hear the echoes of the English of past centuries in contexts that today seem conventional and formal. Official written documents retain features of language such as more complex sentence structures, the choice of more formal vocabulary. Ceremonial language of rituals, such as weddings and funerals, also displays these features, as do letters and essays written by older people, so it can alienate our sympathies, even if there is little problem in understanding. This quote from *The Secret Diary of Adrian Mole*, by Sue Townsend, is a humorous example of this illogical view:

I read a bit of *Pride and Prejudice*, but it was very old-fashioned. I think Jane Austen should write something a bit more modern.

Activity 13 asks you to modernise an extract, not to 'improve' it, but so that you can see some significant changes over time.

ACTIVITY 13

Read this extract from *Rasselas*, by Samuel Johnson, written in 1759.

- Re-write it using more modern expression.

- What changes do you notice to lexical choice and sentence structure?

Now read the commentary on pages 109–110.

(The beginning of Chapter VII, after a failed attempt to construct wings and fly.)

The prince was not much afflicted by this disaster, having suffered himself to hope for a happier event, only because he had no other means of escape in view. He still persisted in his design to leave the happy valley by the first opportunity.

His imagination was now at a stand; he had no prospect of entering into the world; and, notwithstanding all his endeavours to support himself, discontent by degrees preyed upon him, and he began again to lose his thoughts in sadness, when the rainy season, which in these countries is periodical, made it inconvenient to wander in the woods.

What changes and how?

This section looks at each of the language levels in turn.

Phonology (pronunciation changes)

If you listen to a BBC broadcast from the 1950s or 1960s, you will notice differences in pronunciation. It used to be considered 'correct' to pronounce words beginning with 'wh' with an aspirated 'h' sound at the start, but it is rare to hear this now. Try substituting the sound 'ep' for 'ap' in the utterance, 'I'm so happy' and it will sound like an earlier 'posh' pronunciation. There are some noticeable changes in pronunciation today, for example the trend towards a form of pronunciation termed **Estuary English** (see page 109).

Graphology (spelling, punctuation and layout changes)

The trend in spelling changes seems to be towards simplification. The English spelling system is notoriously tricky, as sounds are not consistently represented by combinations of letters. In American English the following simplifications are accepted:

colour, humour, glamour	→ color, humor, glamor
programme	→ program
centre	→ center
organise	→ organize

Other simplifications are found in advertising:

night	→ nite

These changes have had some effect on British spelling, because of the influence of American culture, especially computer technology.

The use of capital and lower-case letters has undergone some change recently. Lower case is used now for names of organisations, particularly if they are connected with the internet, for example lastminute.com. Capital letters are now used in the middle of words for company names, for example HarperCollins.

Punctuation conventions have changed slightly: dashes are used more often today in the place of semi-colons or full stops. The mark for a full stop is now used to punctuate internet addresses, as are slashes and the sign @, for example www.helpme@instantessays/english.co.uk

Morphology (changes in word formation)

This is the most obvious aspect of language change. Every year a dictionary of new words is published in the attempt to keep up with and record new words and phrases coming into the language. The term **neologism** refers to new words. A few are completely fresh inventions, but most are formed from the existing word stock in various ways. The examples should make the labels clear.

- **borrowing** – tandoori
- **compounding** – laptop
- derivation – re-boot (prefix); bootable (suffix)
- **acronym** – DVD
- **blending** – vegeburger (vegetable hamburger)
- **clipping** – mike (microphone)
- changing word class – I need to reformat that.

ACTIVITY 14

Skim through a dictionary of new words and look at the table below.

- Which class of word is most common? (noun, verb, adjective, adverb, other)

- Suggest reasons why this is the case.

- Find examples of other word classes.

- What aspects of society do they refer to?

- Are the words completely new?

- If not, how have they been formed from existing words?

Now read the commentary on pages 110–111.

The following words are taken from *The Oxford Dictionary of New Words*, 1997.

Nouns	Adjectives	Verbs	Prefix
attitude	ambient	cherry-pick	e-
dweeb	bog-standard	download	hyper-
crustie	bootable	get a life	info-
geek	challenged	kick-start	nano-
luvvy	happy-clappy	mosh	mega-
max (to the max)	feel-good	out	of-
road rage	gob-smacked	power nap	
smiley	hardcore	reboot	**Suffix**
yoof	in-your-face	veg	-ware
	loved-up	zap	-watch
Interjection	phat		
not	pull-down	**Adverbs**	
	retro	drop-dead	
	smart	way	
	sorted	well	
	stonking		
	stressed out		
	sussed		
	to-die-for		
	touchy-feely		
	wired		

This term 'neologism' means new word formation, but not all new words formed become part of the language. They may be used for a few years and then drop out of use. It is easy to work out the meaning of new words because we understand the rules for their formation. The term 'MacJob' for example refers to the fast-food chain, McDonald's, and is understood to mean any low-paid, low-skilled job.

Lewis Carroll, the author of *Alice's Adventures in Wonderland*, invented many words, some of which have become part of the language, for example 'chortle' is a blend of the words 'chuckle' and 'snort'. He makes the morphology clear in the following extract where Alice meets the Mock Turtle and the Gryphon:

'Reeling and Writhing ... and then the different branches of Arithmetic – Ambition, Distraction, Uglification and Derision.'

'I never heard of "Uglification",' Alice ventured to say. 'What is it?'

[...]

'You know what to beautify is, I suppose?'

'Yes,' said Alice doubtfully: 'it means – to – make – anything – prettier.'

Activity 15 looks at an example of neologisms from *Brave New World*, by Aldous Huxley, 1932. The extract from *The BFG* by Roald Dahl on pages 68–69 also contains some examples. There may be other examples in the texts you are studying.

ACTIVITY 15   **C3.2**

Read the extracts from *The BFG* on pages 68–69 and *Brave New World* below.

- Identify the neologisms.

- Explain how they have been formed, using the terms at the top of page 77.

Now read the commentary on pages 111–112.

'Bokanovsky's Process is one of the major instruments of social stability!'

[...]

Standard men and women; in uniform batches. The whole of a small factory staffed with the products of a single bokanovskified egg.

[...]

'If we could bokanovskify indefinitely the whole problem would be solved.'

[...]

'Going to the Feelies this evening, Henry?'

[...]

'Try to realise what it was like to have a viviparous mother.'

In a future society, there will be a need for new words for new things and concepts. The same is true of an imaginary society, as in *Alice's Adventures in Wonderland*, *The BFG* and *Brave New World*. It is also true of other societies, such as those portrayed in American novels.

Just as new words come into a language, words disappear from it. The most obvious example is names of things that no longer exist in modern society. There are very few houses today that have a room called a 'parlour' – a smart room reserved for visitors – for example.

Activity 16 gives an example of both of these cases: of words disappearing and of words coming into the language. There may be similar examples in the texts you are studying.

ACTIVITY 16 | C3.2

Read the following extracts from *The Diary of a Nobody*, by George and Weedon Grossmith (1892) and *Brave New World*, by Aldous Huxley (set in a future world).

- Identify words that are unfamiliar.

- Are they disappearing from the language or new words?

- Explain how they have been formed.

Now read the commentary on page 112.

EXTRACT 1

In the dark, I stepped on a piece of the cabbage, which brought me down on the flags all of a heap. For a moment I was stunned, but when I recovered I crawled upstairs into the drawing-room and on looking into the chimney-glass discovered that my chin was bleeding, my shirt smeared with the coal-blocks, and my left trouser torn at the knee.

EXTRACT 2

Swallowed half an hour before closing time, that second dose of *soma* had raised a quite impenetrable wall between the actual universe and their minds. Bottled, they crossed the street; bottled, they took the lift up to Henry's room on the twenty-eighth floor. And yet, bottled as she was, and in spite of that second gramme of *soma*, Lenina did not forget to take all the contraceptive precautions prescribed by the regulations. Years of intensive hypnopaedia and, from twelve to seventeen, Malthusian drill three times a week had made the taking of the precautions almost as automatic and inevitable as blinking.

'Oh, and that reminds me,' she said, as she came back from the bathroom, 'Fanny Crowne wants to know where you found that lovely green morocco-surrogate cartridge belt you gave me.'

Grammar changes

There are fewer changes to the grammatical structure of language and they are not as noticeable as changes to vocabulary (see Activity 14).

Some recent changes are now established in common use. There are few people today who would object to the following structures, which were once considered incorrect:

New structure	Old structure
Who did you see?	Whom did you see?
It's me.	It is I.
Which drawer did you put it in?	In which drawer did you put it?

One change that has become apparent in informal – and fashionable? – use of language is in the use of the word 'so', for example the TV programme in the year 2001: *So Graham Norton*.

The standard use of 'so' is to qualify an adjective: 'I was so happy.' Now it is used to qualify nouns: 'so last year' or even 'That is so not what I wanted.' People can also be heard using 'So?' as a compression of the phrase 'So what?'

Ways of reporting speech have undergone some changes in informal spoken language. Instead of introducing the words with 'he said' or 'she said', you hear phrases like this:

And then *he goes*, 'What do you mean?'
So *she is like*, 'I don't know.'
This is me, 'Are you going then?' *This is him*, 'If you like.'

You may think that this change is restricted to spoken language, possibly only of teenagers. For language change to spread, it needs to be adopted in wider contexts. Perhaps we are witnessing a change in ways of reporting speech, as Activity 17 shows.

ACTIVITY 17

Read the following extracts from *Playstation Zone*, April 1998.

- Note the phrases that report speech.

- Is there any use of formal language in contrast with the colloquial style?

- Do you think this change in grammar will be accepted as standard?

- Who is the intended audience for this text?

Now read the commentary on pages 112–113.

Ben pulled out a drawing of Blasto and we were all just like 'We should do Blasto' [...] All of us were just so sick of video games being dark future post-apocalyptic nightmares and all that stuff and we were like 'pbbbbbt'.

We'd always mimic Blasto and we'd always be like 'It sounds like Phil Hartman' [...]

(They) were all getting very interested in the game and the potential of where it could go, and they were like, 'Let's see if we can get him.' [...]

They showed him Blasto and supposedly he just changed and was like 'Hi, I'm Captain Blasto.'

He calls up and he's all 'Jay, this is Blasto ...' I'm like, 'Oh shit, Mr Hartman, sir, I'm a big fan! ' [...]

I was like, yeah, this is it ...

We were just like hey, maybe we should just collect babes, and then it kind of went to, okay, if he's collecting babes, then each babe's gotta be different ...

A trend, rather than a change, in sentence structure is towards a more informal style, using more simple, compound and minor sentences. One feature of formal styles of writing is the use of complex sentence structures, containing several clauses. You are likely to find more complex sentences in the text you are studying from an earlier period. It is important to be able to identify these structures. First remind yourselves of the explanation given on page 36.

The following example of a complex sentence shows the verbs in each clause in bold type.

> Although I **went** to the pictures **to see** *Star Wars*, we **went** to the pub instead, **having decided** it **was** a waste of money.

The clauses can be bound (as opposed to linked) in two ways:

1   The use of a **subordinating conjunction**: like although, if, who, which, unless, etc. A common subordinating conjunction in English is 'that'. Remember that it can often be omitted:

> This is the person that asked for you.
> I felt sorry (that) I had missed her.
> She said (that) she didn't care.

2   The use of non-finite verb forms. Three are three non-finite forms:

to + verb	*To err* is human
verb + '-ing'	*Peering* through the letterbox, she called his name.
verb + '-ed'	*Exhausted* by the journey, he slept soundly.

ACTIVITY 18

The extract below is taken from *The Diary of a Nobody*, by George and Weedon Grossmith (1892).

- Underline the verbs in each clause and identify the way each clause is either linked or bound together: highlight the conjunctions and non-finite verb forms.

- Try to re-write the extract as a sequence of simple sentences – one verb per sentence.

Now read the commentary on page 113.

In the evening, hearing someone talking in a loud voice to the servant in the downstairs hall, I went out to see who it was, and was surprised to find it was Borset, the butterman, who was both drunk and offensive.

Semantic changes

Words change their meanings in various ways:

- broadening – 'dog' used to be the name for a particular breed of dog, but its meaning now encompasses dogs in general

- narrowing – 'meat' meant food of any kind and 'girl' meant young person of either sex. Now 'meat' refers to animal flesh only and 'girl' is differentiated from 'boy'

- euphemisms – polite terms are created to refer to taboo topics, for example 'lavatory' originally meant a place for washing, but now refers to ... well, all the terms are euphemisms: 'toilet', even 'bog'.

Other words change their meaning to mean something quite different. The word 'cheek' used to mean 'jaw' and vice versa.

ACTIVITY 19

C3.1A

Work in groups.

- How have the following words changed in meaning?

    gay, sad, wicked, black (as in 'Brown is the new black. Black is the new black.')

No commentary.

Discourse changes

Activity 20 looks at the genre of journalism. The article is clearly not a modern newspaper report of a public execution. If you had a photocopy of the original, the graphology would identify it as an old newspaper – much smaller print, everything crammed together more than the modern eye can bear. There are the small give-away details of vocabulary. There may be something about the sentence structure which does not seem contemporary. Before picking out the small details that suggest an earlier style of English, think about the wider issue of discourse. To use an analogy – a friend has spent a fortune and then several hours getting ready for a big occasion: 'How do I look?' If you respond, 'There's a bit of fluff on your hem,' you are missing the main point of the question.

Consider the wider aspects of the discourse of journalism: How would a contemporary article communicate this? What approach would it take? The term 'angle' is often used to describe the writer's point of view. *The Times* newspaper used to be praised for unbiased, factual reporting. It's a popular myth, however, that broadsheet newspapers offer a more factual, unbiased view than tabloids, which offer a more personal, close-up view. If you read a broadsheet newspaper report of a shocking event, you will see that there is a lot of emotional colouring and opinions. Even in the eighteenth century, *The Times* did not maintain a dispassionate view.

ACTIVITY 20   C3.2

Read this article from *The Times*, 23 October 1793. (The word 'ci-devant' means a person who used to be important, but is no longer.) Discuss the following questions in small groups.

- How would a modern newspaper report such an event?
- At what points in the article did you feel more interested and involved?
- Pick out examples of emotional, personal and subjective viewpoints.
- Find contrasts from the other sections of the article.
- What aspects of journalism remain similar today?
- What differences can you identify?

Now read the commentary on pages 113–114.

MARIE ANTOINETTE GUILLOTINED

DIGNITY ON THE SCAFFOLD

Wednesday, October 23, 1793.
Execution of the Queen of France. It is with sincere regret we confirm the general report of yesterday respecting the fate of this unfortunate princess, who suffered under the axe of the guillotine on Wednesday last the 16th instant; after having been condemned on the preceding day by the National Convention as guilty of having been accessary to and having cooperated in different manoeuvres against the liberty of France.

The execution took place at half past eleven o'clock in the forenoon. The whole armed force in Paris was on foot from the Palace of Justice to the Place de la Revolution. The streets were lined by two very close rows of armed citizens. As soon as the ci-devant Queen left the Conciergerie to ascend the scaffold the multitude which was assembled in the courts and the streets cried out *bravo* in the midst of plaudits. Marie Antoinette had on a white loose dress and her hands were tied behind her back. She looked firmly round her on all sides. She was accompanied by the ci-devant curate of St Landry, a Constitutional priest, and on the scaffold preserved her natural dignity of mind.

After the execution three young persons dipped their handkerchiefs in her blood. They were immediately arrested.

ACTIVITY 21

Consider the overall approach / discourse of the earlier text you are studying.

- Does it pose problems for you as a modern reader?

- Try to identify differences in approach – sometimes earlier texts appear too 'leisurely' or detached, for example.

No commentary.

Pragmatic changes

Here are two definitions of pragmatics:

> Pragmatics is the study of how more gets communicated than is said. (Yule, 1996, quoted in J. S. Peccei, *Pragmatics*, 1999)

> Pragmatics can be usefully defined as the study of how utterances have meanings in situations. (Leech, 1983, quoted in J. S. Peccei, *Pragmatics*, 1999)

The emphasis is not so much on what the sentence means, as on what the speaker *means* when they utter it. When you are reading dialogue in novels, there will be some changes over time in the ways in which speakers imply meanings. How to be polite, for example, changes over time and social context. Terms of address such as 'madam' and 'sir' are used less often these days, but it would be a mistake to assume that a speaker from an earlier era was being over-polite, or patronising by using these terms.

ACTIVITY 22

Read this extract from *Brave New World*, by Aldous Huxley.

- What is the implied meaning of 'everybody's happy now'?

- What clues are given in the context to suggest an alternative reading of this statement?

Now read the commentary on page 114.

'What a marvellous switchback!' Lenina laughed delightedly.
 But Henry's tone was almost, for a moment, melancholy. 'Do you know what that switchback was?' he said. 'It was some human being finally and definitely disappearing. Going up in a squirt of hot gas. It would be curious to know what it was – a man or a woman, an Alpha or an Epsilon ...' He sighed. Then, in a resolutely cheerful voice, 'Anyhow,' he concluded, 'there's one thing we can be certain of; whoever he may have been, he was happy when he was alive. Everybody's happy now.'
 'Yes, everybody's happy now,' echoed Lenina. They had heard the words repeated a hundred and fifty times every night for twelve years.

Analysing narrative structure

What is a narrative?

The dictionary definition of *narrative* is, 'a spoken or written account of connected events'. This is obviously very similar to the definition of a *story*. However, a narrative is one particular telling of a story with a particular audience in mind. The events may be roughly the same, but the emphasis and slant will create a very different narrative.

In everyday life, accounts of events also differ for various reasons. Even in court when a witness pledges to tell 'the truth, the whole truth and nothing but the truth', the proceedings would grind to a halt if anyone attempted to tell the 'whole truth'. It is necessary to select the details which are relevant to the situation and each person's choice will give a different emphasis. Assuming that everyone is being honest, each person can still only say what they believed happened. The accounts may then be different because each person witnesses the events from a slightly different viewpoint.

In many novels, the story, or plot, is the main focus for the reader, who wants to find out what happened next. The emphasis in the study of literature, however, is not simply on the *events*, but on the *account*, i.e. *how* the writer chose to present the events.

So, in your analysis of narrative structure, you should consider all three aspects:

teller	story	audience
narrator	plot	reader

Story / plot

You can begin with the storyline, or plot. Some people claim that there are only between seven and twelve plots, which are treated in different ways by novelists, scriptwriters and playwrights. Examples are:

- quest
- rescue
- temptation
- forbidden love
- adventure
- escape
- metamorphosis
- sacrifice.
- pursuit
- revenge
- maturation

The novelist Janni Howker suggests that there are only three or four basic structures that underlie all stories and provides a diagram to represent each.

The relationship
This represents the meeting of the life paths of two strangers and the episodes that follow. Love stories such as *Romeo and Juliet* follow this plot structure. The reader is kept wondering about the outcome of their meeting.

The invited / uninvited guest
Stories with this structure explore how an existing circle of people is affected by the arrival of a stranger. The reader wonders whether the outsider will be integrated into the group, destroy it or be ejected. Many science-fiction, horror and crime stories have this structure, as did the story of Beowulf's struggles with Grendel.

The quest
The diagram shows the ditches and hurdles that make stories about quests interesting. The film story of Indiana Jones follows this pattern.

Perhaps reduction to three patterns is too simple to account for all stories. Certainly complex narratives may include two or more plot strands. *Sir Gawain and the Green Knight*, for example, begins with an uninvited guest pattern, but becomes a quest. However, it is an interesting exercise to try to represent plot structure in diagrammatic form.

You should also consider the *themes* of the text you are studying. Although the ideas and issues are likely to be too complex to express in a single word, the following suggestions may help you to identify something which is at stake for the main characters:

- rivalry
- maturity
- revenge
- power
- love
- death
- jealousy
- life
- hate
- trust.

Audience / reader

As you read, you may be aware that there is an assumed audience for the text that is different from you in important ways. This may cause problems for you as a reader. If you can identify the intended audience, you may understand any difficulties you have in appreciating the text.

One obvious problem occurs when we read texts from other historical periods, because we are distanced from the concerns and conventions of that time. Being able to identify the differences in language, style and overall structure of the text is one of the main Assessment Objectives for this module.

However, there are other ways in which the assumed audience may be different from you, as the actual reader. You may be studying a book for children or young teenagers, for example. (In Module 3 you may decide to write a story for a younger audience.)

The preface to *Alice's Adventures in Wonderland* is a poem by Lewis Carroll, which describes the relationship between teller, tale and audience.

Alice! a childish story take,
And with a gentle hand
Lay it where Childhood's dreams are twined
In Memory's mystic band,
Like pilgrim's wither'd wreath of flowers
Pluck'd in a far-off land.

The audience is not straightforward, however. Lewis Carroll first told the story to a particular girl on a boating trip and later produced a book enjoyed by a wider audience. As an adult he tries to access the world of 'childhood's dreams' through memory. Perhaps his adult perspective succeeded more for adults than children. The book certainly has a dual appeal. There are some comments that would delight an adult readership and baffle a child. The same is true of some comments in *The BFG*, by Roald Dahl. It is important to bear in mind the fact that children's books need to appeal to the adults who purchase and read them, as well as to the children.

The use of language may reflect the needs of children by being simpler in some ways. But it is the themes and ideas that must appeal to the child – or the child in everyone. The Harry Potter books, for example, are extremely popular and are enjoyed by people of all ages.

ACTIVITY 23

C3.1A

Work in small groups.

• List books and stories that you enjoyed as a child.

• Add books that you know younger children enjoy today.

• Do the books have anything in common? Think about:

    – storyline
    – themes
    – characters
    – style of language.

• Did you read *Alice's Adventures in Wonderland* as a child, or have it read to you? What do you remember about it? Did you enjoy it, or was it an adult choice?

• Which Roald Dahl stories have you read or seen in TV / film adaptations? Can you explain their appeal?

Now read the commentary on pages 114–115.

Writing for children

Children's stories are written by adults. The writer tries to identify with what children feel and how they think. Children don't explain to the adult world; they don't leave written records; as they grow up, they allow themselves to forget the intensity of their feelings. From a mature perspective, it's comforting to remember childhood as innocent, simple, sweet, safe. Children's stories that work are not innocent, simple or sweet, but the child usually ends up safe. Adult books can end in death and despair, but that is taboo for children's stories. Perhaps this is because adults can detach themselves and say, 'It's just a story', while children feel the power of stories that communicate real fears – they need to counteract this by ending with hope.

ACTIVITY 24   **C3.1A**   **C3.1B**

Discuss in small groups.

- Which of these feelings do you remember from your childhood?

    - I'm lost / alone.
    - I'm frightened.
    - Who am I?
    - This is strange.
    - Suppose there's a monster under the bed.
    - I hope everything will turn out OK.
    - I wish I could fly / be invisible.
    - I wish my cat / teddy could talk back to me.
    - Food! If only everything was edible.

- Tell a brief anecdote about one or two of these childhood memories.

No commentary.

Narrator / teller

In narratives, it is important to be aware of the *point of view*. In literary criticism, this term does not have the meaning of 'opinion', but refers to the particular *perspective* (position and distance) from which the events are viewed. The events may be related from the perspective of an outsider, or from that of one of the characters involved in the situation.

In *The Secret Diary of Adrian Mole*, by Sue Townsend, for example, the events are narrated by a teenage boy. His view is amusingly restricted – he doesn't understand the significance of some of the things happening around him. As readers, we are aware of this and often make our own, different interpretations of the story he is telling. This kind of narrator is called a **flawed narrator** or 'unreliable narrator'.

Other stories are narrated from the point of view of a character who is presented as more 'reliable', an **omniscient narrator**.

External perspective

If there is an 'outsider' narrator, they may be invisible to the reader and so their account might *appear* to be authoritative, simply recording the facts in a neutral way. The following Zen Buddhist tale has an apparently objective narration:

> Two monks, Tanzan and Ekido, were once travelling together down a muddy road. A heavy rain was falling. Coming around a bend, they met a young girl in a silk kimono and sash, unable to cross the intersection.
>
> 'Come on, girl,' said Tanzan at once. Lifting her in his arms, he carried her over the mud.
>
> Ekido did not speak again until that night when they reached a lodging temple. Then he could no longer restrain himself. 'We monks don't go near females,' he told Tanzan, 'especially not young and lovely ones. It is dangerous. Why did you do that?'
>
> 'I left the girl there,' said Tanzan. 'Are you still carrying her?'

You should still regard this type of narration as a particular point of view. The narration is sympathetic to Tanzan and critical of Ekido. The reader certainly interprets the behaviour of Tanzan in a positive way and Ekido's reaction as obsessive. The narrative expresses certain attitudes and values. This particular example is a fable with a moral message, but you should be aware of the attitudes and values expressed in any narrative and understand how they were created and conveyed. As the reader / audience, you are encouraged to share the attitudes and values of the writer, as probably happened in the fable. It is possible to feel at odds with / alienated from the assumed values.

Activity 25 explores the different ways the story of Tanzan and Ekido could be told to shape the reader's response to the events.

ACTIVITY 25	C3.3

Work in groups. Each person should re-write the events of the story above from a different perspective:

1 Tanzan's 1st-person account, showing him in a less positive light

2 a 3rd-person account, but less sympathetic to Tanzan

3 Ekido's 1st-person account, showing him in a more positive light

4 a 3rd-person account, but more sympathetic to Ekido

5 the girl's 1st-person account.

Read each other's versions and comment on the ways the writer influenced the reader's response to the characters.

No commentary.

Omniscient narrator

Even if the narration appears to come from outside the characters in the story, the narrator need not remain silent and invisible. There may be comments addressed directly to the readers, as in the opening to Jane Austen's novel, *Emma*:

> The real evils indeed of Emma's situation were the power of having rather too much her own way, and a disposition to think a little too well of herself; these were the disadvantages which threatened alloy to her many enjoyments. The danger, however, was at present so unperceived, that they did not by any means rank as misfortunes with her.

These comments sound authoritative, as if from an older wiser person who knows the character well, so the reader accepts them. In fact, all the later events confirm this opinion of Emma.

This need not be the case. You may read texts where you cannot accept the judgements made, or implied, by the narrator. You might resist the assumptions expressed in the following extracts from a traditional Serbian tale:

> The shepherd followed his master's advice and [...] he soon became the richest man in the district. He was so rich in fact that the local squire was glad to accept him as a son-in-law. His young wife was beautiful, but very headstrong. At first the simple shepherd was too impressed by her superior education to notice her faults.

The story of magic and talking animals ends on this cheerful note:

> 'Just listen, my good woman. If you still insist on knowing why I laughed, I shall beat the living daylights out of you.'
>   Needless to say his wife instantly stopped her nagging and what's more, she never nagged again and they lived happily ever after.

Flawed narrator

Some narratives use what is termed a 'flawed narrator' whose judgements are framed as faulty. As readers, we are unlikely to share the opinion of the barber admiring the cruel jokes of his friend Jim, from *The Haircut*, by O. Henry.

Jim had a great trick that he used to play when he was travellin'. For instance he'd be riding on a train and they'd come into some little town like, well, like, we'll say like Benton. Jim would look out the train window and read the signs on the stores. For instance, there'd be a sign, 'Henry Smith, Dry Goods'. Well, Jim would write down the name and the name of the town and when he got to wherever he was going he'd mail back a postal card to Henry Smith at Benton and not sign no name to it, but he'd write on the card, well, somethin' like, 'Ask your wife about that book agent that spent the afternoon last week,' or, 'Ask your missus who kept her from getting lonesome the last time you was in Carterville.' And he'd sign the card 'A Friend.'

Of course, he never knew what really come of none of these jokes, but he could picture what probably happened and that was enough. He certainly was a caution.

ACTIVITY 26

In the following extract from *Alice's Adventures in Wonderland*, by Lewis Carroll, some direct comments from the narrator to the audience are made obvious by the graphology – the use of brackets.

- What is the point of the direct comments?

- Now read the commentary on page 115.

Down, down, down. Would the fall *never* come to an end! 'I wonder how many miles I've fallen by this time?' she said aloud. 'I must be getting somewhere near the centre of the earth. Let me see: that would be four thousand miles down, I think' – (for, you see, Alice had learned several things of this sort in her lessons in the school-room, and though this was not a *very* good opportunity for showing off her knowledge, as there was no one to listen to her, still it was good practice to say it over – 'yes, that's about the right distance – but then I wonder what Latitude or Longitude I've got to?' (Alice had not the slightest idea what Latitude was, or Longitude either, but thought they were nice grand words to say.)

Presently she began again. 'I wonder if I shall fall right *through* the earth! How funny it'll seem to come out among the people that walk with their heads downwards! The Antipathies, I think' – (she was rather glad there *was* no one listening, this time, as it didn't sound at all the right word) – 'but I shall have to ask them what the name of the country is, you know. Please Ma'am, is this New Zealand or Australia?' (and she tried to curtsey as she spoke – fancy *curtseying* as you're falling through the air! Do you think you could manage it?)

ACTIVITY 27

Identify the point of view of the two texts you are studying.

- Are they narrated from the perspective of one of the characters?

- Is this character a 'reliable' narrator?

- Are they narrated from an outsider perspective?

- Are there comments made explicitly by the narrator?

- Assess the attitudes and values implied in the two texts you are studying.

No commentary.

Types of narrative voice

When the narrative is presented from the perspective of one of the characters involved, there are still some choices available to the writer.

3rd person	1st person
he / she / it / they	I / we

1st-person narrative / voice

1st-person narratives create a *flavour* of the style of the character, though this is crafted by the writer. This sense of *narrative voice* allows the reader to adopt an attitude towards the narrator and this influences the way the reader reacts to the story the narrator is telling. Some 1st-person narrators seem so likeable and reliable that they carry the reader along with their version of events. Other narrators are created as less reliable witnesses / characters, so that the reader feels slightly wary of their version of events. Occasionally, the narrator's account is so obviously flawed that the reader must re-interpret their version of events. Such characters are termed 'unreliable / flawed narrators' (see pages 88 and 90).

ACTIVITY 28

Read the following three extracts.

- How do you visualise the narrator in each – gender, age, personality, background?

- Identify features that give a flavour of the narrator's voice, i.e. indicate the aspects of character above.

- Rate the reliability of each narrator on a scale of 1–10.

Now read the commentary on page 115.

EXTRACT 1 (*The Loneliness of the Long Distance Runner*, by Alan Sillitoe)

So as soon as I tell myself that I'm the first man ever to be dropped into the world, and as soon as I take that first flying leap out into the frost grass of an early morning when even birds haven't the heart to whistle, I get to thinking, and that's what I like. I go my rounds in a dream, turning at lane or footpath corners without knowing I'm turning, leaping brooks without knowing they're there, and shouting good morning to the early cow-milker without seeing him. It's a treat, being a long-distance runner, out in the world by yourself with not a soul to make you badtempered or tell you what to do or that there's a shop to break and enter a bit back from the next street.

EXTRACT 2 (*Small Avalanches*, by Joyce Carol Oates)

I ran higher up the hill, off to the side where it was steeper. Little rocks and things came loose and rolled back down. My breath was coming so fast it made me wonder if something was wrong. Down behind me the man was following, stooped over, looking at me, and his hand was pressed against the front of his shirt. I could see his hand moving up and down because he was breathing so hard. I could even see his tongue moving around the edge of his dried out lips ... I started to get afraid and then the tingling came back into me, beginning in my tongue and going out through my whole body, and I couldn't help giggling.

EXTRACT 3 (*The Vet's Daughter*, by Barbara Comyns)

A man with small eyes and a ginger moustache came and spoke to me when I was thinking of something else. Together we walked down a street that was lined with privet hedges. He told me his wife belonged to the Plymouth Brethren, and I said I was sorry because that is what he seemed to need me to say and I saw he was a poor broken-down sort of creature. If he had been a horse, he would have most likely worn kneecaps. We came to a great red railway arch that crossed the road like a heavy rainbow; and near this arch there was a vet's house with a lamp outside. I said, 'You must excuse me,' and left this poor man among the privet hedges.

I entered the house. It was my home and it smelt of animals, although there was lino on the floor. In the brown hall my mother was standing; and she looked at me with her sad eyes half-covered by their heavy lids, but did not speak. She just stood there. Her bones were small and her shoulders sloped; her teeth were not straight either; so, if she had been a dog, my father would have destroyed her. I said, 'Mother, I smell cabbage. It must be lunchtime.'

ACTIVITY 29

Are the texts you are studying written in the voice of a 1st-person narrator?

* Choose an extract and analyse the features that convey aspects of the character.

No commentary.

3rd-person narrative

A **3rd-person** narrative can adopt a style that resembles the character's voice, or it may show events from the character's perspective, but not related in the way that the character would write or speak.

ACTIVITY 30

Read the following extract from *Stone Boy*, by Gina Berriault.

* From whose perspective is the scene related?

* Are the events related in the style / voice of that character?

Now read the commentary on page 115.

Arnold pressed down the bottom wire, thrust a leg through and leaned forward to bring the other leg after. His rifle caught on the wire and he jerked at it. The air was rocked by the sound of the shot. Feeling foolish, he lifted his face, baring it to an expected shower of derision from his brother. But Eugie did not turn around. Instead, from his crouching position, he fell to his knees and then pitched forward onto his face. The ducks rose up crying from the lake, cleared the mountain background and beat away northward across the pale sky.

Arnold squatted beside his brother. Eugie seemed to be climbing the earth, as if the earth ran up and down, and when he found he couldn't scale it he lay still.
'Eugie?'

Then Arnold saw it, under the tendril of hair at the nape of the neck – a slow rising of bright blood. It had an obnoxious movement, like that of a parasite.

ACTIVITY 31

The following extract from *The New Dress*, by Virginia Woolf, is also written in the 3rd person, but it includes colloquial features that suggest the voice of the character Mabel.

- Identify phrases that capture the flavour of her *speaking* voice.

- Identify phrases that seem more like the style of an outside narrator.

Now read the commentary on page 115.

> Mabel had her first serious suspicion that something was wrong as she took her cloak off ...
>
> But she dared not look in the glass. She could not face the whole horror – the pale yellow, idiotically old-fashioned silk dress with its long skirt and its high sleeves and its waist and all the things that looked so charming in the fashion book, but not on her, not among all these ordinary people. She felt like a dressmaker's dummy standing there for young people to stick pins into.
>
> 'But, my dear, it's perfectly charming!' Rose Shaw said, looking her up and down with that little satirical pucker of the lips which she expected – Rose herself being dressed in the height of the fashion, precisely like everybody else, always.
>
> 'We are all like flies trying to crawl over the edge of the saucer,' Mabel thought and repeated the phrase as if she were crossing herself, as if she were trying to find some spell to annul this pain, to make this agony endurable.

Representation of speech (and thought)

Narratives often contain a mixture of descriptions of action and dialogue. The writer can choose to represent what people say (and think) in a variety of ways. Each of the ways of representing speech discussed below creates a different effect. You can see how it affects the reader's perspective, as it draws the reader closer to or further away from the characters.

Narrator summary of speech / thought

A conversation can be summed up and described briefly by the narrator (**narrator summary of speech**) without recording the actual words spoken:

> They argued about it for the rest of the evening.

Thoughts can be recorded in a similar way:

> She couldn't stop thinking about their argument.

The situation has been weighed up and summarised for the reader. The narrator is in control and there is no sense of a character's voice.

Free direct speech

Some writers, for example James Joyce and Roddy Doyle, record dialogues rather like a drama script, simply putting the words spoken on separate lines (**free direct speech**):

> – It is a terrible shame. How can he behave like that?
> – You tell me.

This is a more external style of narration. The reader is left to interpret the tone of voice.

Direct speech / thought

The most common way of representing speech, however, is to record the words spoken inside speech marks, with some indication of who was speaking:

> 'It is a terrible shame,' Pat said. 'How can he behave like that?'

Thoughts are sometimes recorded in this way, even though it is artificial – we rarely think in organised sentences:

> 'It is a terrible shame,' Pat thought.

When **direct speech** is used, the writer has the technical problem of repetition. To avoid repeating the word 'said', *synonyms* are often used. The choice of words can indicate tone of voice:

> exclaimed / whispered / ordered

An adverb or adverbial phrase can add interpretation of mood and feelings:

> with rising panic / scornfully / wistfully

The reader is provided with an internal viewpoint of the characters' minds.

Indirect speech

Words can be reported by the narrator as **indirect speech**. There are some grammatical changes to the form of the words in these cases. There is an introductory reporting clause; the verb changes to the past tense and the pronouns change to 3rd person, for example.

Direct speech	Indirect speech
'I need to have a rest,' she said.	She said (that) she needed to have a rest.
'It's a terrible shame,' Pat said.	Pat said (that) that was a terrible shame.

As indirect speech is the narrator's summary, there is less sense of the character's voice.

Free indirect speech

Sometimes the words can be reported in the past tense but without an introductory reporting clause like 'she said'. This representation of speech is called **free indirect speech**. Its grammatical structure is similar to a narrative description or comment:

That was a terrible shame. How could he do such a thing?

It is no longer ambiguous, however, if some colloquial features are included to keep as much of the flavour of the speaking voice as possible:

Oooh, that was a terrible shame! How could he do something like that?

Although the words are not presented directly, the reader feels closer to the character, than in indirect speech.

ACTIVITY 32

This extract is from the short story, *Rope*, by Katherine Anne Porter. Read the opening paragraphs of the story. A young couple are bickering about the rope that the husband bought from the village shop. The writer uses a variety of ways of representing their argument.

- Find examples of:
    - indirect speech (his and hers)
    - free indirect speech (his and hers)
    - free direct speech (his and hers). Look for sentences where the verb is still in the present tense
    - narrator summary of action.

- Where are you placed as a reader – neutral observer / sympathetic to him / to her?

- Re-write the conversation in direct speech.

- How does this change the effect?

- Add verbs or other phrases to indicate the tone of voice.

Now read the commentary on page 116.

On the third day after they moved to the country he came walking back from the village carrying a basket of groceries and a twenty-four-yard coil of rope. She came out to meet him, wiping her hands on her green smock. Her hair was tumbled, her nose was scarlet with sunburn; he told her that already she looked like a born country woman. His grey flannel shirt stuck to him, his heavy shoes were dusty. She assured him he looked like a rural character in a play.

Had he brought the coffee? She had been waiting all day long for coffee. They had forgot it when they ordered at the store the first day.

Gosh, no, he hadn't. Lord, now he'd have to go back. Yes, he would if it killed him. He thought, though, he had everything else. She reminded him it was only because he didn't drink coffee himself. If he did he would remember it quick enough. Suppose they ran out of cigarettes? Then she saw the rope. What was that for? Well, he thought it might do to hang clothes on, or something. Naturally she asked him if he thought they were going to run a laundry? They already had a fifty-foot line hanging right before his eyes. Why, hadn't he noticed it, really? It was a blot on the landscape to her.

He thought there were a lot of things a rope might come in handy for. She wanted to know what, for instance. He thought a few seconds but nothing occurred. They could wait and see, couldn't they? You need all sorts of strange odds and ends around a place in the country. She said, yes, that was so; but she thought just at that time, when every penny counted, it seemed funny to buy more rope. That was all. She hadn't meant anything else. She hadn't just seen, not at first, why he felt it was necessary.

Well, thunder, he had bought it because he wanted to, and that was all there was to it. She thought that was reason enough, and couldn't understand why he hadn't said so at first. Undoubtedly it would be useful, twenty-four yards of rope, there were hundreds of things – she couldn't think of any at the moment – but it would come in. Of course. As he had said, things always did in the country.

But she was a little disappointed about the coffee, and oh, look, look, look at the eggs! Oh, my, they're all running! What had he put on top of them? Hadn't he known eggs mustn't be squeezed? Squeezed, who had squeezed them, he wanted to know. What a silly thing to say. He had simply brought them along in the basket with the other things. If they got broke it was the grocer's fault. He should know better than to put heavy things on top of eggs.

Bringing it all together

In the exam, you will have an extract from each of your texts on which to focus your analysis.

- You will be discussing the ways that themes, ideas, attitudes and values are presented.

- You should relate these to your understanding of the texts as a whole.

- You should show awareness of changes in language over time or different social contexts.

The following activities are based on extracts from *The Diary of a Nobody*, by George and Weedon Grossmith and *The Secret Diary of Adrian Mole*, by Sue Townsend.

Idiolect

ACTIVITY 33

Read the two extracts and assess the idiolect of the 1st-person narrators.

- Write a pen portrait of each 'I' character. How do you visualise this person – gender, age, social background, era, personality, appearance, speaking voice?

- Compare with a partner.

- Report back similarities. Were there any significant differences?

- Explain the similarities by reference to the text.

- Justify your different interpretations.

Read the commentary on page 117, before doing the next activity.

EXTRACT 1

APRIL 6. Eggs for breakfast simply shocking; sent them back to Borset with my compliments, and he needn't call any more for orders. Couldn't find umbrella, and though it was pouring with rain, had to go without it. Sarah said Mr Gowing must have took it by mistake last night, as there was a stick in the 'all that didn't belong to nobody. In the evening, hearing someone talking in a loud voice to the servant in the downstairs hall, I went out to see who it was, and was surprised to find it was Borset, the butterman, who was both drunk and offensive. Borset, on seeing me, said he would be hanged if he would ever serve City clerks any more – the game wasn't worth the candle. I restrained my feelings, and quietly remarked that I thought it was possible for a City clerk to be a *gentleman*. He replied he was very glad to hear it, and wanted to know whether I had ever come across one, for *he* hadn't. He left the house, slamming the door after him, which nearly broke the fanlight; and I heard him fall over the scraper, which made me feel glad I hadn't removed it. When he had gone, I thought of a splendid answer I ought to have given him. However, I will keep it for another occasion.

EXTRACT 2

Saturday April 4th

NEW MOON

Me and my father cleaned the house up today. We had no choice: my grandma is coming for tea tomorrow. We went to Sainsbury's in the afternoon. My father chose a trolley that was impossible to steer. It also squeaked as if somebody was torturing mice. I was ashamed to be heard with it. My father chose food that is bad for you. I had to put my foot down and insist that he bought some fresh fruit and salad. When we got to the check-out he couldn't find his banker's card, the cashier wouldn't take a cheque without it, so the supervisor had to come and stop the argument. I had to lend my father some of my birthday money. So he owes me eight pounds thirty-eight and a half pence. I made him write an IOU on the back of the till roll.

But I must say that I take my hat off to Sainsbury's, they seem to attract a better class of person. I saw a vicar choosing toilet paper; he chose a four-roll pack of purple three-ply. He must have money to burn! He could have bought some shiny white and given the difference to the poor. What a hypocrite!

Language change

As you saw in Activity 14, language change is most noticeable in the nouns which come into the language to cope with the changing paraphernalia of society of the time. Similarly nouns drop out of use, as the things they describe are no longer part of life.

ACTIVITY 34

- Pick out the nouns from each extract that reflect the society of the time.

Now read the commentary on pages 117–118.

Another aspect of language that changes rapidly is the expressions used to express approval or disapproval. These will also change between social groups at any one time. Adrian Mole's choice of phrase may already seem dated to you: 'dead good', 'a bit of a drag', 'dead lucky', 'absolutely fantastic'.

ACTIVITY 35

Identify the phrases that Henry Pooter uses to express approval and disapproval.

- Pick out any idioms that sound dated.

- Notice the ones which are metaphors.

Now read the commentary on page 118.

Discourse / genre

The diary form allows a quick change of topic, without having to provide elegant links. It can be used in autobiographical, factual writing, for example the diaries of Samuel Pepys, written in the seventeenth century.

The fictional use of diary form can be used in narratives for serious purposes. A psychological thriller might use this device to allow a glimpse of the workings of a psychopathic mind, for example *The Collector*, by John Fowles. Diary entries were used to chart the emotional development of the teenage characters in *A Message for the Pigman*, by Paul Zindel.

There are many other examples of the diary form used for humour, for example *Bridget Jones's Diary*, by Helen Fielding.

The main characteristic of the style of this genre is that it is written in brief, clipped sentences. The writer gets to the point without including grammatical words that add little to the sense. The omission of grammatical words is a feature of any condensed form of language – notices, headlines, postcards, etc. This type of abbreviation is called **ellipsis**. The sentence structure is termed minor. Pronouns, auxiliary verbs and determiners can be omitted.

Often the subject pronoun 'I' is omitted, as there is no need to keep repeating it:

(I) went to the pictures.

Auxiliary verbs can be left out:

(Have) gone to the shops. (Do you) want anything?

The verb 'to be' can also be omitted, as the sense can be worked out without it:

New *Star Wars* film (was) a complete waste of money.

Determiners can also be omitted, as above and below:

Met (my) friend in (the) pub.

The Secret Diary of Adrian Mole generally uses full sentences, but sometimes the entry begins with a minor sentence: 'Had a postcard from my mother.' This is presumably to give a flavour of a diary style, without writing entirely in note form, which the reader might find too flat and disjointed.

ACTIVITY 36

Read the extract from *The Diary of a Nobody* on page 99 again.

- Is it written entirely in minor sentences?
- Write down any sentences that are abbreviated.
- Show which words have been omitted and label them.

Now read the commentary on page 118.

Pragmatics

The diary form is used in these texts as a comic device. It captures the voice of a particular individual, who, in both cases, takes himself very seriously. The gap between the impression they think they are creating and the one conveyed is one source of humour. The writers portray their absorption in their small triumphs in an exaggerated way that seems ridiculous. (For Module 3 you might try creating a comic persona either in diary form – to be read – or as a monologue – to be listened to.)

Grice's maxims of conversation

The philosopher, Paul Grice, suggested that conversation works on a **co-operative principle**. The participants keep to certain conventions so that conversation works well. Two of **Grice's maxims** are useful for analysing Mr Pooter's anecdotes:

- the maxim of Quantity says that you should provide neither too much, nor too little information

- the maxim of Relevance is that you keep your comments relevant.

A dull person usually gives listeners / readers far more information than they require. Conversely, interesting details may be omitted. They may also choose to explain things of dubious interest / relevance. Although this diary is not a conversation, Mr Pooter is addressing his readers in such a way that we would be bored and irritated, if we didn't find the fictional version amusing. He is flouting the maxims of Quantity and Relevance.

ACTIVITY 37	**C3.3**

- How does Mr Pooter flout the maxims of Quantity and Relevance?

- Write another episode of his diary:

  - choose topics of dubious interest and give a little too much detail
  - use minor sentences at the beginning, at least, to imitate the style of diary form
  - use very restrained, 'proper' vocabulary.

Now read the commentary on page 118.

Your study of prose texts in this module has introduced some linguistic concepts concerning language change and some literary concepts about the creation of perspective and point of view. You will have noticed, however, that it is hard to maintain an absolute distinction between literary and linguistic concepts: when analysing perspective, for example, you looked at the linguistic features of indirect speech. These concepts will be useful to you if you choose to produce a narrative in Module 3. Together with the concepts introduced in Module 1 for the study of the anthology and poetry, the concepts studied in this module provide a basis for Language and Literature study at A2 Level.

Commentaries

Activity 1

Vocabulary and meanings. Only the first two are considered archaic in *Chambers English Dictionary* (1998):

apparrelled	clothed (archaic)
meat	food (archaic)

The others are certainly not in common usage, but are not listed as archaic – yet:

polled	shorn (cut hair)
sloth	laziness
stripe	blow with a lash

There is also an unusual use of a preposition:

Receive money *of* a serving-man   *from* a serving-man

Verb forms.

needeth / cometh / hireth	needs / comes / hires
cheaper than he should hire	could
every one of them be apparrelled	is apparrelled
their heads be not polled	are not polled

Word order.

for so be these ... called	for this is how these ... are called
And no less jeopardy it is	And it is no less dangerous

Activity 2

The first is Dorothy Wordsworth's entry for 10 June 1802. The second is Kenneth Williams's entry for 14 June 1962. There are clues to the historical period in the references to Coleridge (a nineteenth-century poet) and Billy Graham (a twentieth-century evangelist), but there seems little change over 160 years – in diary-writing style, at least.

'William very poorly' and 'Went to park' are minor (abbreviated) sentence structures typically used in diaries. This can also be called *ellipsis*, which literally means 'leaving out' – the verb is left out of the first sentence and the subject of the second. These are both texts written originally for a private audience, so it may be that this aspect of context has a greater influence on choice of style than the historical period. Of course, the language will also reflect the style of a particular individual.

The language of both may have seemed a little old-fashioned, but could be examples of contemporary English, perhaps written by an elderly person.

1 The use of capital letters for some common nouns (Books, Branch) in the first does not follow modern conventions, nor does the use of a hyphen in 'sack-full'. The conventions for spelling compound words like this usually go through stages: first two single words (word processor), then hyphenated (word-processor), and finally a single word (wordprocessor). You will notice that 'sittingroom' is spelt as a single word. The adjective 'poorly' is used in some regional dialects of English.

2 You might not have thought the expression 'receiving their kissings & caressings' was unusual; in fact, the computer spellcheck objects to the two nouns formed from the verbs 'kiss' and 'caress'. This change of word class is a common way of forming new words (see Activity 14), but the attitudes probably seemed old-fashioned or very refined, particularly the notion expressed in the slang term 'riff-raff'.

Activity 3

The letter was printed on Wednesday, 2 August 2000. It is by Count Nicolai Tolstoy, who refers to himself as the son of an immigrant. It is likely that the group dated it as much earlier text. Certain uses of vocabulary seem old-fashioned:

I had occasion
the paper dispenser
impeccable hand
lapidary dictum

'Lapidary' means inscribed in stone and 'dictum' is a saying. Neither word is said to be archaic in a contemporary dictionary, but both are rarely used. The structure of the opening sentence is complex with a subordinate clause:

while conducting researches

Adverbial phrases are used at the beginning of sentences:

Several years ago
Above the paper dispenser

The overall impression is of a very formal, complex style, which is not so common these days.

However, it is misleading to say that 'language has changed' full stop. It is in a state of flux. Writing in many situations these days tends towards a more informal choice of vocabulary; less complex sentence structure; more direct address from writer to reader. Some groups of language users accept these changes and other groups resist them (see page 74).

There is a tendency for speakers of English as their second language to retain more formal elements of style. If you learn a language from books, your exposure is to written forms and, because of the time lapse in publishing, these may not be the contemporary forms. It is also safer for learners to stick with established forms, as it takes time to see whether new expressions are a passing fashion or here to stay.

Activity 4

The register has all the features of formal academic style, with one long, complex sentence that includes **polysyllabic**, abstract, Latinate vocabulary.

The prize was for The World's Worst Writing Competition from the journal *Philosophy and Literature*, 1998. It is an annual contest to celebrate 'the most stylistically lamentable passages found in scholarly books and articles'.

As a reader, you probably found this text simultaneously incomprehensible and impressive, but you might have been amused by the cruel prize it was awarded. To be fair, the audience for this text may have had few problems with it. It is from an article in an academic journal, so only other experts in the field would choose to read it. If the author were writing a textbook for school students on Cultural Studies, they would adapt their language; if they were writing a novel to entertain a wide audience, they would use a quite different style.

Activity 5

1 This is the difference v. deficit debate: although some people regard regional dialects as inferior to SE, linguists recognise that there are many different varieties of English over the world and do not assign superiority to one particular variety. It would seem that the further the speaker is from the centres of power (London, Edinburgh, Dublin), the less prestige their accent has. In the media, regional accents are sometimes used in stereotypical ways to portray lovable, but slightly thick rogues. Research into attitudes towards regional accents show that listeners tend to assess the speakers as less intelligent, but more trustworthy, brave and friendly.

2 The English spelling system does not accurately represent the pronunciation of any accent, yet spelling is only distorted for regional accents, making them look peculiar and comic on the page. One exception to this is the cartoonist, Steve Bell, who portrays the more 'powerful' accents of royals and politicians in distorted spelling:

    I viry much admire also your civil nuclyah pah praygrem.

    High exectly do you make a pair of trizers? Do you ekshly sew them together on thet machine? High many trizers do you make a day?

    However, only a few words have been changed, otherwise it might be impossible to read.

3 The use of a regional accent is often associated with membership of a lower social class.

Activity 6

The use of vocabulary is standard with some familiar colloquial phrases, which might seem slightly dated: 'snatch of tune ... twiddly bits'. However, the man's choice of word to express approval – 'topping' – is not in use today.

The only change in standard spelling to indicate pronunciation is ''ud', but the shortening of 'she would' to 'she'd' is not restricted to any particular region of the country. Such elision is common in speech and is often represented in writing. The unusual spelling suggests there's something different about the way the man pronounces it.

There is grammatical variation in the verb forms and the pronouns.

Non-standard dialect	Standard dialect (SE)
Mary were thee sang / set her 'ud / must / sought Any new song that come out	Mary was you sang / put she would / must / sought Any new song that came out

Activity 7

1 Huck lives in the southern state of Missouri in the United States in the late nineteenth century. Brought up by a drunken father, he has had little formal education. He is about thirteen years old. His grammar differs from Standard British English and also from the standard grammar of the widow.

Huck's dialect	Standard British English
The widow she cried she never meant no harm She put me in them new clothes feel all cramped up The widow rung a bell there warn't really anything	The widow cried she never meant any harm She put me in those new clothes feel cramped up The widow rang a bell there wasn't really anything

There are some vocabulary choices which are not Standard British English, but may have been standard in the United States at the time:

come to time / go right to eating / grumble a little over the victuals

There are no changes to the spelling to indicate Huck's pronunciation.

2 Jim also lives in Missouri in the late nineteenth century. As a negro slave, he would have had little, if any, formal education. There is some debate about the portrayal of Jim. Some feel that it is racist. Certainly there are so many spelling changes, it's virtually unreadable and so could create irritation on the part of the reader.

Activity 8

The Giant uses non-standard verb forms, but the use is not identified with any particular region, nor is it consistent. The verb forms are changed and occasionally pronouns are changed.

Standard English	Giant dialect
I am	I is hungry!
You are	You is about right!
They *do* gobble	They *does* gobble up human beans!
We are	We is in Giant Country now!
We have	Out there us has the famous Bonecrunching Giant!
... are all tasting / all taste	Greeks from Greece is all tasting greasy.

But it's not consistent, as the story continues:

> As I am (is) saying ...
> I collect (is collecting) them ...
> You are (is) once again gobblefunking!
> Giant crunches (is crunching) up two ...
> They say (is saying) the ...

This style of speech gives the Giant a distinctive manner of speaking and makes him seem friendly and harmless. The heroine's SE distinguishes her as human and, perhaps, more educated than the Giant.

Activity 9

Extract 1 is a model essay from a book called *Modern English* by John Russell, produced for secondary school students in the 1930s.

Extract 2 is an article from the Sri Lankan *Daily News*, 4 September 2000.

Extract 3 is an article from the sports pages of the *Guardian*, 2 October 2000.

Many people would guess that Extracts 1 and 2 were written in similar periods much earlier than Extract 3. The historical context is just one of many influences on language. There are other important factors of context: social and cultural; spoken or written mode; genre; purpose and audience.

English is spoken in Sri Lanka by people who see it as an important means and sign of social advancement. It is formally taught, often at private elocution lessons. The models of the English language tend to be written texts, either literature or essays. These factors will lead to the use of a more formal style of English.

The textbook's purpose was to teach a standard form of writing compositions and essays in order to pass school exams, at a time when it was accepted that education should promote a 'correct' model of speaking and writing.

The article by 'Darren Tackle' in the sports section is intended to appeal to football fans who are likely to be amused by the use of contemporary slang and jargon.

The first two extracts use SE, some dated words and structures and therefore a relatively formal style:

> I walked forth …
> to allow of our having
> to behold
> I ventured to try it, …
> get its fingers soiled
> Hunger sharpened by a little of the glass that cheers

Extract 3 uses non-standard grammar and vocabulary, including modern slang, so seems very informal and possibly ill-educated?

Non-standard grammar	Standard English	Slang
I has not seen What with … there is not enough hours What can afford to be go all patriotic get hisself	I have not Because of … there are not that / which can become very patriotic get himself	posh geezer

Activity 10

List 1. In natural speech, most people drop one of the consonant sounds (often 't'), when there is an awkward cluster of consonants:

> pos(t)card, foo(–)ball, ho(–) water bottle, singin(–) a song

In fact, the following are now the accepted pronunciation:

> fas(–)en, cas(–)le, han(–)kerchief

Some people pronounce 'often' with a 't' sound; others omit it. If your partner is not convinced, ask them to say the words 'prints' and 'prince' in a sentence and see if you can hear a difference in pronunciation, for example:

> The Prince asked for his prints back.

List 2. We naturally add sounds to make the transition between sounds easier:

> ham-p-ster, Ne-y-ul, Ga-y-ul, draw-r-ing, Sue w-and me, India r-and Pakistan

List 3. Sometimes people drop vowel sounds in words like these:

> ev(e)ry, fact(o)ry, nurs(e)ry, fam(i)ly, choc(o)late

Activity 11

1 and 2. These are examples where the standard form is irregular, but the regular form still exists. The words 'hisself' and 'theirselves' are used in some regional dialects, but are considered non-standard. In fact they were probably the original forms:

I	me	my	myself
you	you	your	yourself
she	her	her	herself
he	him	his	hisself / himself
we	us	our	ourselves
they	them	their	theirselves / themselves

3, 4 and 5. The situation is similar to that of Chinese Whispers, where the sounds are not distinct and the hearer repeats their best guess, thus 'He might've gone' becomes 'He might of gone'; 'She's seen it' becomes 'She seen it'; 'a napron' becomes 'an apron'. The first two are considered non-standard, but – like an apron – they may become the accepted use.

6. The plural form of 'brother' has become regular, although the older form exists in more formal contexts.

7, 8, 9 and 10. The long vowel in the first word becomes a short vowel in the second, perhaps because it is easier to pronounce. It happens in so many cases, for example senile → senility and serene → serenity, that regularity may be another cause.

Activity 12

Fashion. Terms to express approval and disapproval change quickly. In the 1960s, things were 'swinging' or 'dodgy'; in the 1980s they were 'ace'. The term 'pants' was declining in popular use in the year 2000.

Contact with others. There are noticeable changes in pronunciation by influential and popular media stars, for example Paul Merton and Jonathan Ross in the year 2000. The term 'Estuary English' refers to this type of pronunciation, which is a modified version of RP, that may drop 'aitches' and use glottal stops instead of the plosive consonant 't', for example 'I haven'(–) go(–) a lo(–)'. It is likely that this form of pronunciation will spread and that RP will decline. Received Pronunciation was regarded as the prestige accent and a passport to a good job. At one time, it was the accent used by all BBC announcers. Now a very small percentage of people speak with an RP accent and it no longer has the same prestige. In some ways it is seen as a handicap. The journalist, Boris Johnson, felt that he had lost his job presenting a radio programme because of his 'posh' accent and said defensively, 'We plummy voiced brayers can adapt.'

Need. It is interesting to see the origins of words for new technology – few are completely new, but are formed from existing words (see Activity 12). New names for existing things often put a fresh spin on them, for example names for 'trousers': slacks, pants, cords, jeans, chinos. You can probably add the latest ways of naming this item of clothing.

Activity 13

Here is an example of how the first paragraph might be modernised:

The prince wasn't badly affected by this set-back, even though he had hoped it would succeed, because he hadn't got any other ideas for a way of escaping. He was still determined to get out of the happy valley as soon as possible.

Your re-writing probably changed structures that sound dated, such as 'having suffered himself to' and 'notwithstanding all his endeavours'. In the second paragraph, the original sentence is very long for the conventions of modern English prose style. (A computer grammar check would point this out.) You may have used full stops, rather than semi-colons.

If you omitted vocabulary such as 'persisted', 'endeavours', and used words such as 'kept', 'tried', the change can be described in various ways. You have moved from:

polysyllabic to monosyllabic
more formal to more informal
Latinate to Old English or Norse origins (see page 32)

None of the vocabulary or sentence structures is archaic, strictly speaking. However, Samuel Johnson's style seems dated to a modern reader in some aspects, i.e. it uses vocabulary and structures that are no longer in common use. Other vocabulary and structures seem formal, i.e. more likely to be used in impersonal writing for a wide audience. The two terms – dated and formal – overlap as the use of dated, or archaic, terms tends to make the style seem formal. The notion of a scale of styles (or registers), ranging from very formal and impersonal to very informal and intimate, is based partly on the effect on the audience, but also on observable features of language.

Activity 14

More than 90% of new words are nouns. The words are often names for modern phenomena:

- food products – decaf
- technology – hacker
- fashion – goth
- music – gabba.

There are fewer adjectives and verbs. Although there are clearly new things that need to be referred to, modern life does not produce so many new qualities or new actions. A look at new adjectives reveals that they often have near synonyms: 'phat' means excellent, in a sense, except that the precise word chosen to express approval or disapproval also conveys the speaker's age group and social background. These new words tend to last only as long as the fashion season. 'Swinging' was a 1960s word, replaced swiftly by 'ace', 'magic' and 'wicked': 'phat' may be obsolete by the time this book is printed.

The only completely new word formations are 'stonking', 'sussed' and 'phat'. Often an existing word is used in a different sense, like 'sorted'. Other words are formed from existing words, like 'bootable'. Many are compound words, like 'bog-standard', with some triple combinations like 'in-your-face'.

The small number of new verbs are often formed from existing words and also appear to put a new spin on existing concepts: 'power-napping' sounds grander than 'having a snooze'. There are words for new activities, however, particularly in the field of computers and dance.

There were only three new adverbs in this edition of the dictionary. All three are used as intensifiers (see page 26), with the same function as 'very', but a very different effect. If you had just read the words 'a way different effect', it would seem strange to use such a modern, colloquial phrase in a formal context such as a textbook. It's the language equivalent of parents and teachers dressed in ripped jeans.

There are no new pronouns, prepositions, conjunctions or determiners. There is one new interjection – 'not!' It was made popular in the Wayne's World sketches on *Saturday Night Live*. Now it is accepted enough to be used by broadsheet newspapers.

There are some new prefixes and suffixes, used mostly in the contexts of technology and marketing.

The term 'SE' refers to the words (and grammatical structures) accepted as the norm. If the new word is the only one that can be used, it is usually accepted as standard. If it is an alternative expression, it may be classed as colloquial or non-standard. The decision about whether something is standard or not is often just a matter of time and attitude. The abbreviation 'fridge' for 'refrigerator' is now accepted as SE, for example.

Activity 15

The BFG. 'Man-gobbling', 'earbursting' and 'uckyslush' are neologisms formed by compounding. The compound 'man-eating' is accepted as standard, but this new word uses the colloquial 'gobbling' instead. Many compounds with the word 'ear' are listed in *Harrap's English Dictionary* (1998) and 'earbursting' may be included one day. To 'earbash' is listed as an Australian colloquialism, meaning to talk incessantly. The standard word 'slush' has been combined with the onomatopoeic 'ucky'; 'crackety-crack' is also explained by onomatopoeia.

'Murderful' and 'glamourly' are formed by derivation. The term 'derivation' refers to the adding of suffixes (or prefixes) to existing words. The neologism 'cannybull' (a word that has been misheard) has then had a suffix added.

The word 'whiffle' is listed in the dictionary meaning to make a slight whistling or puffing sound, so it sounds like a blend of the words whistle and puff.

'Scrumptious' is listed as meaning delicious, but its origin is uncertain. The word 'diddle' has been infixed (placed in the middle rather than the beginning or end) which is unusual.

'Wopsey' is not listed, but suggests the word 'wop' changed into an adjective by the suffix '-y'.

Brave New World. The name Bokanovsky has had its word class changed. It been turned into a verb by adding the suffix '-ify', and then into an adjective by adding '-ified'.

We know the word 'movies' formed from 'moving pictures' (clipping) so we can understand that 'Feelies' are images you can feel.

'Viviparous' is actually an existing word, that was formed from 'vivi-' meaning 'live' and 'parous' meaning 'giving birth'. It was formed by compounding. In the New World society, live birth was the exception, so the use of a rare word shows it was considered unusual.

Activity 16

The Diary of a Nobody. 'Flags' would be called flagstones today, perhaps because they are not so common, so the short form is not enough to make the meaning clear.

The words 'chimney-glass' and 'coal-blocks' are disappearing from the English language, as the things to which they refer are not part of modern life. It is interesting to note that they are compound words, so perhaps formed to describe things that were new at that time.

Brave New World. The unfamiliar words are existing words, though not in common use. The fact that many of them are taken from the fields of science and technology shows the efforts of this future society to control the human and emotional by scientific means.

'*Soma*' means the body of an animal or plant excluding the germ cells, but Aldous Huxley used it as the name of a mind-numbing drug.

'Hypnopaedia' means learning or conditioning by repetition of recorded sound during sleep.

'Malthusian' is formed from the name of Thomas Malthus, a nineteenth-century economist who suggested that the increase of population tends to outstrip the means of living.

'Morocco-surrogate' is a compound word referring to a substitute for goatskin leather.

'Bottled' is a verb formed from the common noun. Is it used today to mean drunk?

Activity 17

Phrases that report speech all use 'x was like ...' with slight variations. Often the adverb 'just' is inserted, also a feature of colloquial language. At one point, the usage is abbreviated to 'he's all (like) ...' There is little use of formal language as a contrast.

The use of non-standard language is intended to appeal to the audience which is likely to be young males – computer-game enthusiasts. The fairly restricted audience means that this use is less likely to become accepted as standard. It would need to be taken up by a wider, or more influential group. Its use in computer-generation novels, such as those by Douglas Coupland (*Generation X, Microserfs, Shampoo Planet*), might have more impact than its use in a magazine read only by young people.

Activity 18

In the evening, <u>hearing</u> someone <u>talking</u> in a loud voice to the servant in the downstairs hall, I went out <u>to see</u> who it <u>was</u>, and <u>was</u> surprised <u>to find</u> it <u>was</u> Borset, the butterman, who <u>was</u> both drunk and offensive.

The re-written version should look something like this:

> In the evening, I heard someone. They were talking in a loud voice to the servant in the downstairs hall. I went out. I wanted to see this person. Who was it? I was surprised. It was Borset, the butterman. I found that out. He was both drunk and offensive.

Activity 20

There is a change in naming the subject of the article, from her official title 'Queen of France' to her personal name 'Marie Antoinette'. The headline chooses the more personal title, perhaps to attract interest, but the opening factual sentence uses her official title. The description of her actions on the scaffold returns to her personal name. This account discreetly stops the description after she looks around with her hands tied behind her. It flashes forward to the gory detail of three people dipping their handkerchiefs in the blood.

The important historical details, such as dates and proper nouns are given. All we know of the man accompanying her is 'ci-devant curate of St Landry, a Constitutional priest'. Other details are not provided in this account, whereas a contemporary newspaper tends to include age to encourage the reader to identify on a more personal level. Tabloid newspapers often include details such as hair colour.

Marie Antoinette's dress is described as 'white loose' and conveys an emotional impact as a metonym for purity and simplicity. There are subjective opinions expressed in the words 'fate', 'unfortunate', 'suffered'. This is the true opinion of the newspaper. But there are interpretations of her state of mind which may or may not be true, for example 'She looked *firmly* round her', for example, 'preserved her natural *dignity* of mind'.

The crowd is described in general terms: 'two very close rows of armed citizens', 'cried out *bravo*'. The sudden close-up of three individuals is much more affecting: 'three young persons dipped their handkerchiefs in her blood.' Modern newspapers often close in on the reaction of individuals and gory details are always powerful.

Although there is something 'dated' about the language of 1793, it is broadly similar to contemporary English. Dating of texts is not as straightforward as the dating of rocks, for example. This is because of the other factors of language variation. The style would be different in an eighteenth-century text written for a different purpose, in a different mode, with a different audience, by a speaker of a different geographical and social dialect. If we had access to recordings of spoken language, there would be another variable.

Activity 22

The implied meaning is that everybody was not happy before, and that although they have been made to be happy, perhaps are not really. The fact that Henry's tone is said to be 'melancholy' opposes the word 'happy', as does the fact of a human 'going up in a squirt of hot gas'. He had to make an effort to be 'resolutely' cheerful and Lenina echoes it in an automatic fashion, that we can read as hollow, rather than emphatic, repetition. This is emphasised by the comment that they had heard it 'repeated a hundred and fifty times every night for twelve years'. That amount of repetition is extreme.

Activity 23

Books that appeal to children tend to have some characteristics in common.

Storyline. Adventure, fantasy.

Themes. Adventure, quest (always ending happily).

Characters. Main character is usually a child that can be identified with. Often away from the safety of parents. Other characters are often animals or fantasy creatures, some friendly despite their strangeness, others presenting a threat. Adults remain shadowy background figures.

Style of language. Inventive, playful, containing neologisms. Is it true to say that the language is 'simple'? It is often so creative that it delights the adult readers as much as the children. The vocabulary is certainly not dry, abstract, formal, nor are the sentence structures over-complex.

Many children's stories take place in another world. This other world is a parallel universe: although strange in some ways, it shares some underlying principles with the familiar world. Access to this world can be gained in various ways – through the back of a wardrobe in C. S. Lewis's Narnia stories; by putting on a garment with special powers, etc. *The BFG* and *Alice's Adventures in Wonderland* suggest it is the world of dreams that each person enters every night of their lives. Sophie's adventures begin at the point of slipping from sleep into waking; Alice's begin at the point of drifting off to sleep. Falling asleep is a strange sensation for children and most have some fears about going to bed, not simply because it is dark and they are alone, but because of the experience of dreaming. Most remember the frightening dreams and need reassurance that they didn't really happen. The worry can't be completely dispelled, though: however bizarre the actual occurrences, the underlying emotion is present in waking life. It is enjoyable and comforting to hear stories that deal with dream adventures. It is likely that these stories would be read to a child by an adult, so there is a link to the safe, ordinary, waking world that adults seem to inhabit. Even if the child reads the story alone, the author's voice is heard at intervals, stopping the complete immersion in the dream world.

Activity 26

The direct comments are not so much about Alice herself, as about children and education. They seem to be addressed to child readers, but they show the gap between a child's knowledge and an adult's understanding, so might be better appreciated by adult readers.

Activity 28

1   The narrator is a teenage boy serving time at a Borstal for theft.

2   The narrator is a young American teenage girl.

3   The narrator is a young woman.

You may have assessed these narrators in decreasing levels of reliability. The reader's sympathies are likely to be with the narrator of the first extract. He describes his feelings vividly. The narrator of the second extract seems rather naïve, not really understanding the significance of the threat that the man poses. Her underlying fear expresses itself in nervous laughter. The narrator of the third extract describes physical surroundings, but seems detached from emotions. Her comments are particularly disjointed when she enters a house and then comments that it was her home. Her comments about the smell of animals and her mother are an odd way of seeing people as animals. Her father seems to pose a threat, which she cannot make explicit.

Activity 30

The extract is related from the perspective of the young boy, Arnold, who has accidentally shot and killed his brother, Eugie. But it is not written in the style that he himself would use, phrases like 'tendril of hair at the nape of the neck', 'It had an obnoxious movement, like that of a parasite' are not those of a young boy. In fact, Arnold is so traumatised by the horror of the situation that he is unable to talk about it at all, hence the title, *Stone Boy*.

Activity 31

Expressions like 'face the whole horror – the pale yellow, idiotically old-fashioned silk dress', 'to stick pins into', 'dressed in the height of fashion, precisely like everybody else, always' are ones that Mabel herself would probably use. The phrase, 'as if she were tryihg to find some spell to annul this pain, to make this agony endurable' seem in the style of an outside narrator.

Activity 32

Indirect speech. 'he **told** her **that** already **she looked** like a born country woman', 'She **assured** him **he looked** like a rural character in a play.'

Compare this with the direct-speech version to see the changes in pronouns and verb tense:

> 'You look like a born country woman,' he told her.

> 'You look like a rural character in a play,' she replied.

Free indirect speech. Had he brought the coffee? She had been waiting all day long for coffee. ... Gosh, no, he hadn't. Lord, now he'd have to go back. Yes, he would if it killed him.

Compare the direct-speech version. You may have added *evaluative verbs*, *adverbs* or *descriptive phrases* to indicate the tone of voice:

> 'Have you brought the coffee? I've been waiting all day long for coffee,' she *complained* (petulantly, with irritation in her voice).

> 'Gosh, no, I haven't. Lord, I'll have to go back now,' he sighed. 'Yes, I will, even if it kills me,' he insisted (sounding fed-up, in a martyred voice).

Free direct speech.

> You need all sorts of strange odds and ends around a place in the country.

> And oh, look, look, look at the eggs! Oh, my, they're all running!

Narrator summary of action. Apart from the first few sentences there are very few narrative descriptions of action:

> Then she saw the rope.

Most of the narrative is in free indirect speech. This gives the *flavour* of their actual words, but with a certain distance, as if we are hearing a lively, but knowing, report of their argument. The perspective moves back and forth between the two, almost like a ping-pong match, so the reader is left equally poised between the two viewpoints. Or perhaps the effect is to make the reader feel stuck in the middle, not always sure who is speaking.

Changing the conversation into direct speech leaves a rather irritating account of their bickering. It is unnecessary to add evaluative comments, as the reader is able to judge the situation and understand all the simmering tension, but is left to wonder what is going on in their relationship to cause such angst about a basket of shopping. There are clues during the story: they are new to the country and finding the unfamiliar life stressful; they are newly married; they are short of money. This is not spelt out to the reader and, presumably, the couple are not fully aware why they are arguing. By the end they have made up and realised how silly it all was, but the reader suspects it may all start again the next day.

Activity 33

1 Middle-aged male, respectable aspiring middle-class status, very conventional and polite, rather dull, dressed in a slightly shabby, brown or grey suit, hair neatly combed to cover bald patch, speaks in a slow, quiet voice, pronouncing words carefully. Living at end of nineteenth century.

He disapproves of any show of emotions, is perhaps afraid of anger: 'hearing someone talking in a loud voice', 'the butterman, who was both drunk and offensive', 'He left the house, slamming the door after him'. He is always cautious in the way he behaves and speaks, even when annoyed: 'simply shocking', 'with my compliments', 'I restrained my feelings and quietly remarked'. Only when he is alone later does he think of something more lively to say: 'When he had gone, I thought of a splendid answer I ought to have given him. However, I will keep it for another occasion.' He is the sort of careful person who avoids even the risk of getting wet in the rain: 'Couldn't find umbrella, and though it was pouring with rain, had to go without it.'

2 Fourteen-year-old boy living in the 1980s. Seems middle-class, a bit of a snob and concerned about 'proper' behaviour, so probably neatly dressed in fairly conventional way. Self-conscious manner. Earnest and rather self-righteous sense of right and wrong.

He is a typical teenager, embarrassed by his parents and hating being conspicuous: 'I was ashamed to be heard with it', 'the supervisor had to come and stop the argument.'

He feels generally aggrieved by all the trials that life brings: 'We had no choice', 'that was impossible', 'I had to lend my father'. He is quick to criticise other people: 'What a hypocrite!' His attitudes are rather patronising: 'they seem to attract a better class of person.'

He uses rather 'adult' phrasing when he speaks: 'I had to put my foot down', 'But I must say that I take my hat off to Sainsbury's'.

Activity 34

1 In the 1890s extract there are names for jobs that no longer exist: butterman and city clerk. Although there may be similar occupations, the term 'clerk' is rarely used nowadays, as job titles tend to put a more attractive spin on them. There are also words for household objects that are no longer common: fanlight, scraper. We would not specify downstairs hall today, as there is no upstairs hall in most houses.

2 In the 1980s extract, there are names for things in supermarkets, that may cease to exist or be renamed: trolley, check-out, till roll, and the wonderfully specific category of toilet paper: 'four-roll pack of purple three-ply'. It is very rare to find 'shiny white' types of toilet paper now. Just as cheque books are being replaced by banker's cards, so these may also become obsolete. We now longer have 'half pence' and many people say thirty-eight p, not pence.

There is also noticeable change in colloquial language – especially in catch phrases that express approval or dislike. They change as fast as fashions in clothes and music, perhaps for similar reasons. Adrian Mole uses phrases such as 'a bit of a drag', 'mad about Pandora', 'a boring old brick', 'dead lucky', 'absolutely fantastic', 'clapped-out old rubbish'. Notice that most of these use metaphor.

Activity 35

Pooter uses the following words and phrases to express approval and disapproval: 'splendid', 'simply shocking', 'he would be hanged', 'the game wasn't worth the candle'. They all sound dated. Even 'splendid' is a metaphor, as its original meaning is 'shining brightly'.

Activity 36

It is interesting that the writer begins the diary entry using the typical elliptical style, but returns to full sentences once the style is established. Presumably this is because the text would be too clipped and jerky if it were to continue like this. It is enough to provide the illusion.

(The) Eggs for breakfast (were) simply shocking	determiner and verb 'to be'
(I) sent them back to Borset	pronoun
(I) Couldn't find (my) umbrella	pronoun and determiner
(I) had to go without it	pronoun

Activity 37

Mr Pooter flouts the maxim of Relevance. The quality of breakfast eggs; the mislaying of the umbrella.

Mr Pooter flouts the maxim of Quantity. Reporting in detail what someone else suggested might have happened to the umbrella; the exact phrases used by Borset in a trivial argument; mentioning a brilliant idea, but not saying what it was.

MODULE 3 Production of texts

This module counts for 30% of the AS qualification or 15% of the total A Level marks.

— ASSESSMENT OBJECTIVES —

The skills and knowledge that you develop in this module and that will be assessed in your coursework, are defined by the examination board's Assessment Objectives. These require that you:

1 show understanding of the ways contextual variation and choices of form, style and vocabulary shape the meanings of texts (10% of the final AS mark; 5% of the final A Level mark)

2 identify and consider the ways attitudes and values are created and conveyed in speech and writing (5% of the final AS mark; 2.5% of the final A Level mark)

3 demonstrate expertise and accuracy in writing for a variety of specific purposes and audiences, drawing on knowledge of literary texts and features of language to explain and comment on the choices made (15% of the final AS mark; 7.5% of the final A Level mark).

There is a Chinese proverb that says:

I hear and I forget
I see and I remember
I do and I understand.

How is this relevant to the English Language and Literature course? The first two modules assess the skills of an independent, confident and reflective reader. In a sense, they involve 'hearing and seeing' examples of language and literature. This module assesses the skills of a writer. It is the chance to 'do' some language and literature, and in doing the writing yourself, your understanding of how such texts are produced should develop further.

Content of coursework folder

This coursework module is assessed by a folder, containing two pieces of your own writing, drafts of each, a commentary on each piece and any relevant source material:

- one piece must be written for a reading audience and one piece for a listening audience

- each piece must also be differentiated in its primary purpose, for example one intended to persuade and the other to inform; one intended to instruct and the other to entertain

- the total length of the two pieces should be between 1500 and 3000 words

- the total length of the commentary for both pieces should be under 1500 words

- early drafts must be included to show the development of the final draft

- source material and style models should be included if relevant.

The two final drafts are the focus of the assessment. 50% of the marks are awarded for the writing skills displayed in these two texts and 50% for the commentary on the texts.

It is important to understand exactly what skills are required in this English Language and Literature course. It is not a *specialist* writing course in, say, journalism or poetry. In the study of a range of language and literary texts, you should develop the skills of a *versatile* writer, able to produce a variety of effective texts for both listeners and readers, in different genres and for different purposes.

Although half the marks are awarded for the finished *product*, there is equal credit given for understanding of the *process* of writing. Much of your folder will be taken up with drafts, style models and commentaries. These are not just padding. The early drafts will show the changes made after getting feedback on your initial attempt. The commentary should discuss the problems, choices and decisions made. It is important to include style models, if you were working within a specific genre like computer games magazines, for example, or if you re-presented information from one source for a different audience or genre.

Opportunities for Key Skills

In this module, there are also opportunities to provide evidence for each of the five Key Skills areas. The following skills, in particular, can be demonstrated at Level 3 in the activities in this section:

Communication	
C3.1a	Contribute to discussions
C3.1b	Make a presentation
C3.3	Write different types of documents

The focus of this module is the production of different types of documents. Before making the final choice of two texts to submit in your folder, you will practise writing in a variety of genres, for different purposes. As one of the texts is for a listening audience, you will need to present it orally to test its effectiveness. Discussion of your own and other students' writing is an important part of the re-drafting process.

Information technology	
IT3.1	Plan and select information
IT3.2	Develop information
IT3.3	Present information

When producing a text for readers, you may choose a genre, such as leaflets or magazine articles, that uses visual presentation devices to enhance the text. If you choose to write a text to inform, you may use information technology to search for more detailed information.

Working with others	
WO3.1	Plan the activity
WO3.2	Work towards agreed objectives
WO3.3	Review the activity

As the activities encourage you to treat writing as a craft that can be developed in group work, there will clearly be many opportunities to demonstrate skills in working with others.

Improving own learning and performance	
LP3.1	Agree and plan targets
LP3.2	Seek feedback and support
LP3.3	Review progress

These skills can be demonstrated in your choice of tasks for specific purposes, audiences and genres and the process of drafting in the light of feedback comments. When you produce commentaries, these will include your review of the changes you made and the effectiveness of the final draft.

Problem solving	
PS3.1	Recognise, explain and describe the problem
PS3.2	Generate and compare different ways of solving problems
PS3.3	Plan and implement options
PS3.4	Agree and review approaches to tackling problems

The first draft of a text is rarely completely successful. The ability to identify problems and generate solutions is an essential part of the writing process. It is often helpful to consult others, though the final decision needs to be taken by the writer.

Activities are marked with a Key Skills symbol where relevant, e.g. | IT3.1 |

What are you aiming for in the final drafts?

There is a lot of debate about the qualities of good writing. People often say, 'It's subjective.' If this was the case, you would need to know the personal taste of the examiner and try to write to please them. It is more objective than this, as Activity 1 will show.

ACTIVITY 1   C3.1A

Read the following four texts about mint.

• If you were asked which of these texts is the best, what would you say?

Now read the commentary on page 171.

EXTRACT 1

FRESH HERBS

The use of herbs in cooking is so much a matter of tradition, almost of superstition, that the fact that it is also a question of personal taste is overlooked, and experiments seldom tried; in fact the restriction of this herb to that dish is usually quite arbitrary and because somebody long ago discovered that basil works some sort of spell with tomatoes, fennel with fish, and rosemary with pork, it occurs to few people to reverse the traditional usage; to take an example, fennel is an excellent complement to pork, adding the sharpness which is supplied in English cookery by apple sauce, while basil enhances almost anything with which it is cooked; for ideas one has only to look to the cooking of other countries to see how the use of herbs as a flavouring can be varied. In England mint is considered to have an affinity for lamb, new potatoes, and green peas; the French regard the use of mint as yet another sign of English barbarism, and scarcely ever employ it, while all over the Middle East, where the cooking is uncivilised, mint is one of the most commonly used of herbs; it goes into soups, sauces, omelettes, salads, purees of dried vegetables and into the sweet cooling mint tea drunk by the Persians and Arabs. In Spain, where the cooking has been much influenced by the Arabs, it is also used in stews and soups; it is usually one of the ingredients of the sweet sour sauces which the Italians like, and which are a legacy from the Romans, and in modern Roman cooking wild mint gives a characteristic flavour to stewed mushrooms and vegetable soups. The Indians make a fresh chutney from pounded mint, mangoes, onions and chillies which is an excellent accompaniment to fish and cold meat as well as to curries. Mint is one of the cleanest tasting of herbs and will give a lively tang to many vegetables, carrots, tomatoes, mushrooms, lentils; a little finely chopped mint is good in fish soups and stews, and with braised duck; a cold roast duck served on a bed of freshly picked mint makes a lovely, fresh-smelling summer dish; a few leaves can be added to the orange salad to serve with it. Dried mint is one of the most useful of herbs for the winter, for it greatly enlivens purees and soups, ragouts of meat and vegetables and winter salads of beetroot, potatoes, and other cooked vegetables.

EXTRACT 2

MINT

Mint is a herb which is used in cooking all around the world. Different countries use the flavour of mint with various dishes.

England: lamb, duck, new potatoes, peas.

Italy: mushrooms, vegetable soups, sweet and sour sauces.

Spain: stews, soups.

India: chutney (served with fish, cold meats and curries).

Middle East: sauces, omelettes, salads, pureed vegetables, sweet tea.

EXTRACT 3

HERBS IN THE KITCHEN

This week's top tips for cooking with herbs.

Mint is that favourite old standby for Sunday dinner – mint sauce with lamb, fresh mint as a garnish for new potatoes or peas. But you can also use mint for other meals. Either fresh or dried mint can be used to pep up the flavour of carrots, mushrooms or tomatoes. Perhaps stick with apple sauce for pork and cranberry for turkey, but try using mint with duck. You can add mint to many soups and stews in winter and in summer it makes a lovely addition to salads, particularly one with orange slices in it. If you enjoy curries, there's a delicious Indian chutney made from mint, mangoes, onions and chillies, which can be blended together in your liquidiser.

EXTRACT 4

HOW MUCH OF A STICK-IN-THE-MUD ARE YOU WHEN IT COMES TO COOKING?

(And for those of you whose idea of a good meal is dashing out to the nearest take-away, stop reading now!)

You wouldn't dream of borrowing your dad's old cast-offs, would you, so why pinch dear old mum's tried and tested recipes? If you want to impress your latest – you hope – catch with a home-cooked meal, go for something wild and daring.

Take mint, for example. (And the French, masters of the culinary arts, would do just that and chuck it straight in the bin!) Forget mint sauce with roast lamb and plunge into those oh-so-trendy Middle Eastern flavours. If you're only just past the boil-an-egg stage of cooking, bung a few leaves of fresh mint into an omelette, serve with crusty bread and a bottle of Lebanese red and you've made your reputation. In fact, plenty of mint leaves will transform your boring old English salad into something romantic. At the end of the evening, what about some cooling mint tea, instead of the predictable cup of instant coffee? The possibilities are endless. Abandon the old rules, go by YOUR own taste, experimenting is the name of the game.

The writing process

As the coursework folder assesses the process of writing as well as the finished product, it is important to understand what is involved in the process of writing a text.

Writer's block

The biggest hurdle in writing is the first one – putting the first words on a blank sheet of paper. Nearly every professional writer, as well as student writers, admits to suffering from writer's block, whether it's just a matter of putting it off for a few hours, or being unable to start for months. Why? What is it about writing that causes most people to freeze and find any other task more attractive? The author, Susan Sontag comments, 'Setting out to write, if you have the idea of 'literature' in your head, is formidable, intimidating. A plunge in an icy lake.'

Perhaps you are the sort of person who enjoys writing, but most people feel the pressure of producing something in a permanent form that will be judged. This is unlike the relative ease of speaking, where you can compose your ideas in short bursts as you go along. But if you think of speaking in public, or recording your words for posterity, then the situation becomes difficult in similar ways. 'Stand up, please, in front of the whole class and tell us what you think.' Words which came easily before are frozen. Is the look on their faces pity, boredom or amusement? 'We're going to send a recorded message to your grandmother. Why not tell her all about your holiday? Speak into the microphone now.' Suddenly there is little to say about the holiday. You re-play the tape and feel self-conscious about the sound of your own voice.

ACTIVITY 2   C3.1A

- Write down two or three negative aspects of writing in your experience.

- Add two or three positive points.

- Compare with the rest of the group in a pyramiding exercise (see page 6).

Now read the commentary on page 171.

Getting started

The reasons why people find starting a piece of writing difficult are not as important as the strategies for overcoming it. Often the task seems too big and too vague. It looms ahead 'due in a month or so', so there is no pressing need to take the first step. The following are general principles for making the task seem more do-able.

1 Set yourself smaller goals. Break the task down – write a title, make outline notes, choose a section that is easy to write. (I put off writing this section for four days, then the morning of the fifth day, then another hour.

Finally I wrote the title and went away to make a cup of tea, did a bit of washing up, made a phone call. I sketched in the headings, wrote this first bit of explanation and gave up till the next morning.)

2 Create deadlines for yourself. Set a definite time, so that there is the same sort of commitment as you have to go to work or to a class: 'I will begin at eleven o'clock and write for an hour.' Half an hour, or even fifteen minutes, is better than nothing. Once you have started, the momentum will keep you writing for longer in the next session.

3 Remember that drafting is part of the writer's process. In other words, the first thing you write is not going to be the finished product that you show to other people. Remembering that takes the pressure off you. You can tear up the first draft if there is really nothing worth keeping. But you usually find there *is* something worth keeping and working on.

4 Practise writing. Write little and often. This acts like a warm-up for writing an extended piece.

The following activities are intended as short, one-off exercises, rather than the beginning of something to be developed. It is best to do these exercises in a group, where everyone writes something and the group gives feedback comments to each writer.

ACTIVITY 3 — C3.1A

Imagine a country pub. A man walks in. He is wearing a grey suit, a gold watch and two gold rings on one hand. He has a scar on his cheek. There is a woman with him.

- Write a description of the woman's appearance in five sentences.
- Listen to each person's description of the woman.
- Comment on any interesting similarities and differences.
- Discuss what 'story' is suggested about these two people.

Now read the commentary on pages 171–172.

ACTIVITY 4 — WO3.2 WO3.3

- Imagine a person other than yourself. Do not name or describe the person in any way. This person is walking down a street. They have a bag with them.
  - Write a description of the bag and 5–10 things that are in it.
  - Now write about the street. What does this person see as they walk?
  - As the person begins to run, the bag falls and everything spills on to the ground. What do they pick up first?

- Work in small groups and first listen to each account of what the person sees as they walk.

  - Say what impression you get of that person's character, feelings and background. Was the gender obvious? Where do you imagine they are going and why? The writer can then say whether this is accurate.
  - Next read out the description of the bag and its contents. Does this add to or change your impression of the character?

- Finally, write an account of your person, explaining what the character is like, where they are going and what emotions they feel as they walk.

  - Compare this version with the description you first wrote and say which one you prefer as a reader and why.

Now read the commentary on page 172.

Constructive criticism

Activities 1–4 involved some comment on short pieces of writing. The comments focused on the content, rather than the style, so there was no judgement of the writer involved. Making comments on the style is a risky area, but it cannot be avoided. The process of writing involves a series of attempts at the task, i.e. a series of partial failures! Ideally, the weaknesses in early drafts are gradually ironed out. It is necessary to feel generally pleased with the first attempt, otherwise you would give up and bin it, but the harsh fact is that you need to be able to take a step back and accept that there are problems. It is hard for the writer to do this alone. The writer's most valuable asset is a reliable critic, someone who will give honest feedback without destroying confidence. This is unlikely to be your mother or your best friend. Because writing seems so personal, sometimes even the tutor resorts to vaguely polite praise. This is no use at all – the final draft will still have the crucial weaknesses of the first attempt and the first honest comment will be the mark it is given.

Activity 5 develops the skills of constructive criticism – honest and helpful comments that identify strengths and weaknesses. It is important to establish a workshop situation, where writing is seen as a craft. Everyone, including the tutor if possible, should put themselves on the line by producing a piece of writing and everyone should give and receive comments on the writing.

Before you comment on each other's writing, practise the skills of criticism on the texts that follow. It is easier to make honest comments about an anonymous writer's work. You don't have to worry about preserving their feelings, so you are free to say exactly what you think.

ACTIVITY 5   PS3.1 PS3.2

Read the text for a poster giving advice about coping with bullying. Its purpose is to help students entering secondary school.

- Write down one aspect of the text that is effective in your opinion and one aspect that doesn't work well.

- Begin with the positive comments. See whether others in the group agree with your judgement.

- Move on to the critical comments. Explain why something doesn't work and suggest changes – either to cut it completely or modify it.

Now read the commentary on page 172.

You don't have a clue how I feel.

I've never felt so alone!

This is Martin. He has spent the last two years of his school life feeling **hurt**, **angry**, **helpless** and **weak**. He eats his lunch alone in a quiet corner avoiding lifting his eyes from the floor in case he eggs one of them on.

Martin feels so alone he can't see that someone else may feel like he does.

If you are someone who always seems to be the target for the school bully – you don't have to feel alone!!

Don't spend your life in **dread**!! If you are being bullied, it is time it stopped!!

Call CAB (Concerned about bullying) free on ... for an information pack. This information will – I PROMISE – help you get rid of the bully – forever!!

Let's combat bullying!

You're safe with us

Drafting and commentary

It is important to keep the first draft of any text you will submit in the coursework folder. Try to get feedback from other writers or your target audience. You should also try to read it critically yourself and mark any aspects or phrases that you are not entirely satisfied with. It is easier to do this after a time lapse of a few days, weeks or even months, as you can be more detached and read it with fresh eyes. If the piece is intended for listeners, you will need to read it aloud to see how well the language works 'off the page'. Highlight the areas of your text that you may change, so that a teacher or moderator can see the judgements you were making.

Your second draft will address the problems identified at this stage. It is helpful to highlight these changes in some way and then refer to them in your commentary. You may be satisfied with your text now. In that case, produce a final version without any marks or comments. This is the final draft that will be assessed. If you wish to make further changes, you can include two or three further drafts, each highlighted to show changes, but make sure that the final text is free of marks and comments.

ACTIVITY 6		LP3.2	PS3.3	IT3.3

Produce your own text for a poster giving advice.

- Decide on the topic and your target audience. Think where the poster might be displayed. (Examples of possible topics are 'Personal safety at night' and 'Avoiding theft at festivals'. A topic like 'Managing your money' might not work as a poster.)

- In groups, offer constructive criticism on each other's texts, following the guidelines in Activity 5.

- Re-draft your own text in the light of these comments.

- Write a brief commentary explaining the changes you made to the original.

- Use a word processor to design the layout of the poster, including images.

No commentary.

Mode: Spoken v. written language

In your coursework, you are required to produce one text for a reading audience and one for a listening audience. This means that you will have to show awareness of the differences between spoken and written language, and important areas of overlap.

The following list suggests a spectrum between two extremes.

- spontaneous conversation
- planned monologue

- prepared live talk

- scripted pre-recorded speech

- written representations of speech / dialogue

- written text with colloquial features

- text that uses visual features (lists, diagrams, etc.).

Significant differences

Most of the differences can be accounted for by the different **channels** for communication. The channel is sounds in the case of speech, and marks on a page or screen in the case of writing. (The channel for sign language is gestures.)

Speech has features of accent, stress and intonation, that writing can only suggest by conventions such as non-standard spelling, bold print and capitals.

Speech is often social and interactive, particularly when we are having a conversation. In this case, it is spontaneous in the sense that we need to think on the spot, responding to the other person's contributions. Although it is possible to backtrack and rephrase something, nothing can be unsaid and there is no permanent record, unless someone taped the conversation.

Speech can be planned however, even in conversation, when we have rehearsed something carefully before speaking. This happens more often when we deliver a monologue, even a short answer-phone message.

There is certainly careful planning in the case of a prepared talk or presentation, though there is still a need to think on the spot and respond to the listeners' reactions. If you choose this genre for your folder, you should remember that a talk is not generally delivered word for word from the script (see Activities 9 and 10).

If the talk is to be recorded, it may be read word for word from a script, but the aim is usually to sound like natural speech. This is a less tricky genre for your folder, as it is usually scripted and read word for word.

Although the genre of scripted monologue has a listening audience, there is no feedback and the act of 'speaking' is more accurately 'reading' a written text aloud. Of course, the writer will have kept the audience reactions in mind while preparing and re-drafting the text (see Activity 11).

Representations of dialogue in drama scripts clearly have a listening audience. Short stories may also represent dialogue or the voice of a narrator; this genre is often intended to be read from the page, but some stories are listened to (see Activities 13 and 14).

Written texts such as feature journalism often have features of colloquial language and interaction, even though they would be read silently rather than listened to (see Activities 15–18).

Texts such as leaflets benefit from the use of visual presentation, and may be written in a more detached style (see Activities 21–24).

The piece you submit in your coursework folder aimed at a listening audience will not be spontaneous, or respond to listener feedback – once it has been finished. It is important to remember that your role is that of *writer*, rather than speaker.

Some problems for the writer

The difficulties of writing are expressed in the following account by Harold Rosen.

> The writer is a lonely figure cut off from the stimulus and corrective of listeners. He must be a predictor of reactions and act on his predictions. He writes with one hand tied behind his back, being robbed of gesture. He is robbed too of the tone of his voice and the aid of clues the environment provides. He is condemned to monologue; there is no one to help out, to fill the silences, put words in his mouth, or make encouraging noises.

Rosen portrays the writer as an isolated prisoner to suggest the difficulties of silent one-way communication. This image may seem apt for anyone who has struggled to produce a piece of writing.

However, Rosen's description highlights another problem for writers. Does he also portray writers as male? Once he has used the **noun phrase** 'the writer' to refer to any person who writes, he avoids repeating the phrase by using a pronoun instead. He has chosen the pronoun 'he', but this decision is no longer straightforward. 'He' normally refers to a male individual, but, in the past, it was also accepted as a **generic term**, i.e. the way to refer to people in general, just as the term 'man' was accepted as the generic noun for humans. This can have various effects, as the following statements show.

> Man is a mammal who feeds his young.

The word 'man' is intended to include both males and females, but the second part of the statement sounds odd, as 'his' conjures up a male figure.

> When a police officer has completed his investigation, he files a report.

The problem with this use of 'his' and 'he' is that it may not seem strange; in other words we may accept that police officers are male, not female. This type of use is unfortunate, if our society accepts that police officers may be either female or male. (Note my decision to place the word 'female' first, against the usual tendency.)

If I wish to avoid suggesting that writers are male, I have various options. I can say:

- The writer should re-draft his / her work.

- The writer should re-draft their work.

- The writer should re-draft her work.

- The writer should re-draft its work.

The first option becomes clumsy; the second is considered ungrammatical by some people; the third suggests that writers are female; the last sounds odd. You may notice that I use the second option throughout this section. If you are also faced with this decision in your writing, make sure that you make a conscious choice and can explain it.

Not all writing causes problems, however. It is interesting to note that sending e-mails and text messages causes people much less stress. Perhaps this is because the elements of interaction make it closer to a conversation: messages are often short, a response comes quickly, tone of voice can be conveyed. And spelling and punctuation are not a concern – the writer is not constantly worrying about the appearance of their message.

Before looking at the interesting areas of overlap between spoken and written language, Activity 7 will compare two different modes of language use. The texts exemplify two extreme points on the spectrum above: a spontaneous spoken monologue and a planned written text using visuals.

ACTIVITY 7

Read the two texts. The first is a transcript of someone giving tips to a friend on playing a computer game. (There is no indication of pauses, stress or intonation.) It may help to read it aloud. The second is a printed version of hints for the game.

- Note the main differences in the style and approach.

- Try to explain the differences by referring to the context, e.g:

  – channel
  – degree of planning / forethought
  – possibility for interaction / feedback.

Now read the commentary on pages 172–173.

EXTRACT 1

So go into the main hall and get the clips from the dead zombie on the floor don't go up yet wait till you've got the shotgun or else you've had it keep going through and shoot the dogs official name Cerberus in case you cared when they're running towards you or when they stop for a bit go through to the other room no go through to the map room sorry and don't bother shooting the half-dead zombie official name Cannon Fodder let him bite your feet or walk around him because it's a waste of ammo you can't kill him and go through and get the shotgun always shoot your shotgun as close as you can as it saves on bullets and it's a lot of fun once you've got the shotgun you can go up to the second floor walk along the second floor until you reach the room that's just above the room that's next to the dining room on the first floor do you know what I mean then hang on a minute let me think er kill all the zombies no first kill the one on the right then face the other one and then run behind a statue he'll get stuck and you can kill him at your leisure shoot him no don't shoot him stab him with your C knife and then once he's dead erm just carry on going through basically put the weedkiller in the erm pump thing do you know where the blue crystal is well anyway get that and put that in the tiger statue thing and once you've killed the snake go through the garden and go to the guard house

EXTRACT 2

Floor 1

1 Go through to room 1A.

2 Remember to get the magazine clips from the first of the three corpses.

3 Do not go up the flight of stairs, as you need the shotgun first.

4 Go through the hall, shooting the dogs as they run towards you.

5 Then go through room 1C to the secret map room.

6 Walk round Cannon Fodder zombie and pick up the shotgun.

7 Return to the stairs and go up to F–2.

Floor 2

1 In room 2B, first shoot the zombie on the right.

2 Then hide behind the statue on the left to kill the second zombie.

3 Do not shoot, as the statue will explode, instead use your C knife.

4 Get the weedkiller from 2C and put into the pump in 2A.

5 Find the blue crystal in a chest of drawers in 2D.

6 Put it into the hole in the tiger statue which activates the locked door.

7 Go through, kill the serpent and proceed to the guard house.

Effective use of colloquial features

The previous texts showed two extremes of style and approach – an unscripted spoken explanation and a written tabular version of the instructions. Both worked well for their purposes, but neither would be suitable for inclusion in your folder. The former is chatty and disorganised. The latter is too plain and simple. However, effective texts often use the best of both worlds. Texts for listeners will have more organisation and clarity than spontaneous spoken language. Some texts for readers include features of interaction.

When producing a text to be listened to, you will need to use features of spoken language. It would not be helpful to include mistakes, but some elements of spontaneity and interaction can make a text more interesting for listeners.

Bearing in mind the impossibility of going back over a spoken text, you may use more repetition to help the listener keep track of what they are hearing.

For a scripted talk, for example, you can use verbal features to organise the information more clearly. Instead of visual devices (like the headings and numbered lists in the second text in Activity 7) to signal the structure and organisation of the text, certain words and phrases act as **discourse markers** to help the listener follow the talk:

> First; I'd like to begin by ...
> Another point is; it is also ...
> Moving on; speaking of ...
> To recap; finally; so the important thing ...

You may produce a text for readers that also uses some features of spoken language, such as colloquial vocabulary and minor sentence structures. (These are non-standard in the sense that they are incomplete structures, perhaps beginning with a conjunction. See page 36.) This short extract from the children's book *Way Home* by Libby Hathorn and Gregory Rogers shows how effective these features are in creating a natural spoken voice. Remember that stories for young children are often intended to be read aloud by the adult and listened to by the child. (Sentences 2, 3, and 5 are minor. Colloquial terms are in italics.)

[1]   The cat with no name hears the loud voice of the boy.

[2]   And *way up* there on top of the fence, *this* clever baby *thing* rolls itself up.

[3]   Such a tight little ball of fierce cat.

[4]   It growls and then it spits *right* at the boy called Shane.

[5]   *Mad as anything!*

Although a written text cannot be truly interactive, the use of direct address in interrogatives (questions) or pronouns like 'you' and 'I' establishes a more personal relationship between writer and reader, as this extract from *The Bitch Rules*, by Elizabeth Wurtzel, shows:

I have a dream that some day I will have a daughter who will believe she can eat what she wants, when she wants, without worrying about her thighs or her abs or her butt or the saggy, bat-like arms that some women get at middle age. Maybe she won't even know the word cellulite. Is this too much to expect? I think not. But in the meantime women can stubbornly refuse to succumb to the notion that food is the enemy. The fact is that if you eat what you want, when you want it, and exercise three times a week like the experts say you should, you'll be fine. The whole offensive culture of dieting seems invented as yet another way to make women smaller and weaker – to make us become less, literally. The starving self symbolises a diminishing person, and we ought to strive to be more.

However, the over-use of colloquial features can be a distraction in written texts. Be cautious how you employ the following devices.

The use of 1st- and 2nd-person pronouns (I, we, you) clearly helps to establish a rapport with the reader. But care needs to be taken over the choice of pronoun. 'I' shows that the writer is speaking personally, but this can be surprising if it suddenly appears in the text. If the writer is not a friend or a known person, the reader might wonder who this person is.

'We' can have many references – more than one person writing the text; a group that includes writer and reader; the whole of humankind. It can sound patronising – the 'royal we' is a grand way of referring to the individual speaker. It can mean 'you', as in 'How are we feeling today?'

Although writers can suggest stress and volume by *graphological* conventions such as underlining, bold type, capital letters, italics and exclamation marks, these should be used sparingly. Exclamation marks tend to breed – once the writer uses the first one, every following sentence is an exclamation, then the use escalates to two, even three and sometimes a question mark is added as well!!!? This may work well in a personal letter or e-mail, but seems too excitable, even irritating, in an impersonal written text.

Comments in **parenthesis** establish a relationship between writer and reader, by adding some helpful information or addressing the audience personally. This type of 'aside' is indicated by commas, dashes or brackets:

'My father, as you all know, was in the army.'

'The performance by Bjorn Again – Abba tribute band extraordinaire – was sold out.'

'Scrawling DKNY (Donna Karan New York) on your T-shirt works just as well.'

Again there is a danger of over-use. Too many asides can make the reader lose the thread of the main text. The tone of the comments can irritate if it assumes a relationship that the reader rejects:

(I know what you're thinking!!)

Discourse markers are used in speech to indicate changes in the flow and direction of the conversation:

So, well, now, anyway, right, OK then ...

They are useful for a hint of spontaneity in written texts, but can sound rambling and disorganised, if used too much.

ACTIVITY 8

PS3.1

Comment on the use of colloquial features in the following texts for readers.

Extract 1's purpose is to provide unbiased information in leaflet form to prospective members of a club. The introductory and final paragraphs have been printed.

Extract 2's purpose is to offer advice in a pamphlet for teenagers on interview technique. The opening section has been printed.

- Note the use of personal pronouns, graphological devices, parentheses and discourse markers.

- What effect do they have on the writer–reader relationship?

Now read the commentary on page 173.

EXTRACT 1

Williams Supporters Club

The Williams team has been in motor racing for many years now. Their involvement ranges from Formula One to Touring cars and both of these teams are very successful. Last year we finished second in both the drivers championship and the constructors championship in Formula One but this season our expectations are much higher, we are hoping to win both. At this moment in the season we are in the lead by 40 points in the constructors championship and 21 points in the drivers championship. We would like you to be a part of this but before joining you should know what you get for your money.

    [...]

    When visiting the team, many people expect to see Damon Hill being shaken warmly by the throat but let me assure you that this doesn't happen and the winch on the nose and the spade strapped to the back of Hill's car are just experimental at this stage (just kidding). All of the Williams team are friendly and considered by everyone involved to be just like a family.

    These prices may seem a lot to pay but you do get sent your money's worth.

EXTRACT 2

Preparing for your First Interview

- Well, **you've** now reached the stage where its time to start thinking about that dreaded word ... **INTERVIEWS**!

- Whether it's for university, college, or a job, **I know from experience** that they can be pretty daunting times.

- That's why **I'm here**, to simply go through a few points on how to **improve** your interview technique.

- When **I was** at school **I found** interviews really difficult, but now part of my job is to interview people. There's a **picture of me** on the front page of this pamphlet.

- So, **don't worry**, remember most people find interviews hard, so read on and **we will** go through some **points of interest**.

- You see I'm a local retail manager and so I spend a lot of time interviewing potential employees.

Writing for listeners

Scripted talk

The previous activities looked at some differences between the presentation of information and instruction via the spoken and written word. There are also some important areas of overlap where texts keep the spontaneity and interactive nature of spoken language, but create the clarity and structure that written language can achieve.

The genre of scripted talk can be suitable for inclusion in your folder, particularly if you test it out on the intended audience. There may be opportunities to give an informative talk to fellow students. The problem is that it is not entirely realistic to script the talk word for word. When this happens in some talks and lectures, it often sounds rather stilted. A live talk is usually carefully prepared with headings and notes, which the speaker uses to guide them as they talk more spontaneously on each topic. However, such an outline would not provide sufficiently detailed evidence of your skills in communicating information to listeners. Possible solutions would be to script a talk to be recorded, or to write a full script of your own live talk as a test to guide further drafts. The actual talk could then be recorded and submitted together with the initial script and the final outline of headings and notes.

ACTIVITY 9

- Read this student's script for a talk about extra-curricular activities at Blakeway College. The context is the induction programme for post-16 students entering the college.

  - Note the use of verbal markers to indicate the progression of topics.
  - What colloquial features suggest interaction between speaker and listeners?

- Read the script aloud and record it, if possible.

  - Mark any passages that you think are not effective when spoken.

Now read the commentary on page 174.

Good morning and welcome to Blakeway College. My name is ... and I am here to give you a talk, not on anything related to academics, but on what extra-curricular activities are provided at this college. The purpose of this talk is to make you, the newly enrolled students, aware of what is available in terms of sporting facilities, clubs, trips and societies, not to mention other important opportunities such as careers advice and counselling services.

Firstly, Blakeway College has a long history of sporting excellence with football and rugby teams among the best in the region. Opportunities for joining one of the college's teams are plenty. Try-outs for teams such as football, netball, hockey and rugby usually take place during the first few weeks of the autumn term. Various fixtures are then played against other schools and colleges throughout the year. Sporting facilities provided include a fairly well-equipped gym, basketball courts, netball courts and a multi-purpose field which accommodates football, hockey and rugby. These facilities are made available to all students, irrespective of whether you are a member of a team or not.

Other opportunities are also available at this college and take the form of various clubs and societies. These usually meet after college or during free periods. Clubs at this college range from the chess club for all of you chess masters to the drama club which stages various college productions yearly. Productions in the past include favourites such as *Grease* and *West Side Story*, which have both been huge successes.

Blakeway College has built itself a reputation for housing some of the most active societies in the west. These include the well-known Amnesty International which supports the abolishment of wrongful legal prosecution, slave labour and third world debt. Other societies include the young United Nations. This society, much like the real United Nations, discusses and debates issues affecting various countries around the world. Also the young United Nations from around the west meet yearly for a day conference to represent a chosen country and to discuss global issues.

Apart from clubs and societies, the college also arranges fantastic trips yearly for students. These trips provide opportunities to visit different countries, experience different cultures and make new friends. Trips in the past have included destinations such as France and Italy, the aim being to provide students with a wider cultural spectrum and knowledge than they might otherwise be used to. Also it's a chance for students to have some fun. Trust me. I know.

On a more serious note, Blakeway College provides excellent careers advice. Whether it regards higher education or searching for your future job, a well-qualified careers adviser can help you. They visit the college only twice a week, so if you need to chat with them, appointments can be made via your personal tutor. If, in their absence, you are still thirsty for more information, we have a well-stocked careers section in the main library, which caters for everything you need to know about higher education, training and finding a job.

Lastly, a counselling service is available for all students who require someone to talk to. The service is completely confidential and the college counsellor, Mrs Casey, is very experienced and qualified. So, if you want to talk to someone about how unbearable college is, you can. I've been here a year now, so I know how that feels. Anyway the college counsellor is only in once a week, so appointments can be made with your personal tutor.

Well that's the end of my talk, which is only the tip of the iceberg in terms of opportunities available at this college. I do want to stress one thing: no one will force you to do anything, but take my advice and take up at least one extra-curricular activity. Not only will you meet new people, you will have a chance to do something new and exciting. Thank you for listening and I will be available after the talk to answer any questions you may have. Thanks.

(Imran Nathoo)

ACTIVITY 10   C3.3   C3.1B   LP3.2

1 Write the script for a talk to school students about extra-curricular activities, or a topic of your choice.

  • Produce an outline of the main headings and notes of the content.

  • Write the opening, the way you move from one topic to another and the way the talk ends, in full.

2 Present the talk to others in the group.

  • Get constructive criticism as feedback.

No commentary.

Comedy monologue

This genre can be scripted and read word for word, as it is a monologue to entertain. Much humour comes from playing with language, in particular the recognisable *register* of occupational and social groups. The distinctive patterns of speech are captured and then exaggerated or distorted. Sometimes the humour comes from mixing two registers in an incongruous way. Comedy sketches on radio and TV are often based on this type of humour. Shorter examples from jokes and cartoons demonstrate how quickly the style of language can establish the social context of the speaker:

> A lawyer to his loved one: I love you, Sharon, and these documents will advise you of certain rights you have under federal and state law.

Interviewer: What is the quality you have to get the team going?

Football manager: Belief. Motivation. Motivation, motivation, motivation – the three M's.

Register

The lawyer in the example above was unable to adapt his work style for a more intimate situation. Yet most people are able to adapt their language according to the situation. The term 'register' refers to this type of stylistic variation. It is taken from the field of music, where a piece may be played in a high or low register. It is too simple to say that there are two registers – formal and informal – as the situation can vary in many ways. The factors determining register include:

- whom we are addressing (degree of intimacy or distance)

- whether we are speaking or writing (face to face, on the phone, essay or e-mail)

- what role we are in (at work, socialising)

- what we are trying to achieve (explain, amuse, impress).

The following, for example, are all ways of conveying the message: Do not smoke. You will notice that some would be written and some spoken. There are also degrees of directness, politeness and formality. Which one would you choose for a notice in a student common room?

Stub it out.

No smoking.

Don't smoke here.

Please don't smoke.

Smoking is not allowed.

This is a no-smoking area.

Help us to keep this a smoke-free zone.

Would you respect our no-smoking policy.

Do you realise how dangerous passive smoking is?

Patrons are respectfully reminded that x Council operates a no-smoking policy.

This type of small-scale choice may be important in the text for your folder and should be mentioned in your commentary.

ACTIVITY 11   C3.1A   PS3.1   PS3.2

What (two main) registers can you 'hear' in this text? Give examples of each.

- Pick out examples of incongruous mixing of register.

- Do you feel that it is in bad taste?

- What would you change or cut, if it had to be 100 words shorter?

Now read the commenatary on page 174.

Eulogy – Floozy the hamster (1997–2000)

(With apologies to Earl Spencer)

I stand before you a representative of a class in anguish, a pet corner in denial, and before a school in depression. I would like to thank you all for attending this special gathering in the assembly hall of Rotherham Road Primary School. Many of you have made a special effort to be here today (especially classes D and I, who usually have swimming on a Friday afternoon), because of a need to pay respect to someone close to us all, who we sadly lost in the early hours of Wednesday morning during maths. The very numbers in this hall is a more remarkable tribute to Floozy than I could ever hope to offer her today.

Floozy was the very essence of style, of duty, of racing wheels and beauty. Would anyone here doubt she was the most favoured hamster in the whole of pet corner? All over the school she was a symbol of selflessness, a hope for those truly downtrodden souls whom no one would play with at last break. She devoted her life to being petted by the lonely, forever being taken out of her cage and mauled by members of this school.

Someone with natural class, who proved, during her last month, that she needed no official title of 'Pet for Class A' to pass on her own brand of furry magic.

Today I hope to give thanks for the way she enriched all our lives, even though David Humphries, by stupidly dropping her in the playground, allowed her but half a life. Rather than feeling cheated by David, like Jesus felt by Judas, we must give thanks for the short time we had with Floozy.

There is a temptation to remember you for only your official duties, but, if we do that, we do not acknowledge the very beauty of your character. Your beautiful face with your tickling whiskers, the way you could spin the running wheel faster than any hamster in the cage and your devotion to the babies you reared. I give you the promise that we, the pet corner helpers, will always remember to feed your children as you would have wanted. We will do all we can to continue rearing your babies in the way you started, so they are not merely immersed in duty, but can run and play as you would have wished. We also promise that, under no circumstances, will David Humphries of Class N be allowed to sign out a pet again.

The public image of Floozy as a popular, but independent hamster did not show the full extent of her character. Beneath the official duties lay an insecure hamster living in fear of rejection. The withdrawal of her title 'Pet of Class A' left her traumatised – all she would do was run around on her wheel. Her desire to make those with whom no one would play (such as Billy Jacob) feel loved was fuelled by a deep sense of unworthiness of which her incontinence was merely a symptom.

This vulnerability was sensed by most of the school and reserved her a place even more firmly in our hearts. Her light burns on and, in the words of Steps 'It's one for sorrow, ain't it two too bad'.

The last time I saw Floozy (apart from when she was merely a dollop on the floor) was last Tuesday, when it was my turn to clean out the cages. However smelly it was, I never minded cleaning Floozy's cage, as it was the only time we had together, when she was not surrounded by tons of screaming Infants all wanting to pet her. These are the times I will treasure.

One thing neither of us ever understood was why someone who brought such happiness to many was sneered at by a few. They seemed to find her toilet problem more interesting than the genuine support she gave to people in this school. Some, especially Harry Field and his disciples, thought that writing 'Poozy Floozy' across the pet corner sign would make them look hard. It is my opinion that these cruel people should be punished and punished now!

It seems strange that a hamster given a name meaning to be loving and flirtatious would be tormented in such a cruel way.

I would like everybody to put their hands together as we say our daily prayers and ask God to take care of our deceased pet. We should all give thanks that we were given the opportunity to know a hamster I am proud to call my friend, the unique, the complex, the irreplaceable Floozy, who gave so much and asked for so little in return.

She will never be extinguished from our minds. Amen.

(Joanne Stray)

Choice of character

When you choose a character for a parody, it needs to be a social or occupational register that you are familiar with, either personally or from TV / media representations. There is usually an element of mockery, so it is likely that you will portray a type that you find annoying in some way. The following groups are often the target of humorous parodies, but you should be able to add more examples:

- New Age therapist
- politician
- police or parking warden
- game-show host
- Radio 1 DJ
- holiday rep
- art critic
- small-town shop owner.

If you want to add an element of the bizarre or surreal, try using an incongruous clash of registers:

- the devil welcoming people to hell as if to a business conference
- tour guide showing people round a building site / war zone
- a firefighter quarrelling like an infant about using equipment.

ACTIVITY 12 C3.3 LP3.2

Choose a character from a recognisable social or occupational group and write a comic monologue.

- In groups, read each one and identify the register used.
- Offer constructive criticism, beginning with the aspects that worked well.
- Re-draft a short section in light of the feedback.

No commentary.

Writing stories for readers or listeners

Stories can be written for listeners or readers. Many children's stories are designed to be read aloud by an adult and enjoyed by the child, who listens and looks at the pictures. (Remember, however, that the writer would not be expected to produce the illustrations; it is certainly not an appropriate task for this syllabus.) There is a revival of oral storytelling sessions in pubs now, but these are never read from the page, or even from memory, as a degree of spontaneity is part of the attraction. Recordings of novels on cassette are also popular, as are adaptations of stories on the radio, such as *Book at Bedtime* on Radio 4. Even when reading a story from the page, there is a sense in which we hear a voice, particularly in the representations of speech and dialogue. For these reasons, the genre of short story is included in this section on writing for listeners, but a short story could equally be targeted at a reading audience.

Elements of a story

In your coursework, you are restricted to 3000 words in total for two pieces of writing, so the story must be small scale. A short story is like a 'snapshot', compared with the 'blockbuster film' of many novels. It is important not to rely on a series of dramatic events, as the story will seem two-dimensional and unconvincing. It's not necessary, either, to have a 'twist in the tale'. So, what elements do all stories have?

A beginning, a middle and an end.

This still leaves questions about *when* to begin and end. Some stories begin with waking up and end with going to sleep, but this chronology can seem too predictable. In her short story *Happy Endings*, Margaret Atwood has this to say:

> The only authentic ending is the one provided here:
>
> John and Mary die. John and Mary die. John and Mary die.
>
> So much for endings. Beginnings are always more fun. True connoisseurs, however, are known to favour the stretch in between, since it's the hardest to do anything with.
>
> That's about all that can be said for plots, which anyway are just one thing after another, a what and a what and a what.
>
> Now try How and Why.

Margaret Atwood's comment still leaves questions about what constitutes the beginning, middle and end of stories. The following two frameworks give more detail and can be applied to even the simplest oral story.

1 Beginning   Meet all characters and problem
   Middle   Problem gets worse – surprise, suspense, tension
   End   Problem is resolved

This second framework offers more detail about the 'middle' of a story:

2 Balance
   Disharmony
   Inciting incident
   Problem
   Resolution

This is a story told by a six-year-old girl:

> Me and my sister were watching TV at home when we saw a big car outside the house. We got in the car and drove to the seaside. We drove right into the sea, but there was a big crocodile. It chased us, but we escaped and came back home.

Although brief, the young girl's story has all the elements. According to the second framework, for example:

Balance: The story begins at home
Disharmony: The stealing of the car to start the adventure
Inciting incident: Driving to somewhere 'other'
Problem: Drive into the sea only to get chased by a crocodile
Resolution: Just as things get hairy, drive home and pretend you never went out

It's a story, but it lacks the elements of How and Why, mentioned by Margaret Atwood. These provide the distinction between a story and a plot.

Story v. plot

According to E. M. Forster in *Aspects of the Novel*, a **story** must have a sequence of events. 'The king died and then the queen died' is a story, because there is the minimum sequence of two events. The reader, or listener, of a story wants to know *what* happens next.

Plot, on the other hand, means a secret plan or design. It involves the listener / reader in a different question: '*Why* did this happen?' In the sequence of two events above, if you connect the first event (the death of the king) with the second event (the death of the queen) and make one action the result of the other, you have a plot. 'The king died and then the queen died of grief.' You can add a touch of suspense by delaying the revelation of the reason: 'The queen died and no one knew why until it was discovered that it was through grief at the death of the king.' Notice that the chronology has been changed, i.e. you do not need to begin with the first event in time.

Perspective / point of view

Stories are sometimes referred to as **narratives**, a concept you studied in your work for Module 2. This term emphasises the dynamics of the event, which involves three elements:

- a teller

- a tale

- a tellee.

The story is the tale and the reader / listener, is the tellee, but it is important to be aware of the narrator, or teller, who can relate the story from various perspectives.

One choice of perspective is external, where the teller is not present as a character in the story, but describes the scene and the events in ways similar to film and other visual media. With **external narration**, the reader is enabled to visualise the scene, seeing the characters from a distance or moving in close to them, hearing their speech and pausing on certain details:

The television screen was blank. Matt sat in the armchair staring at it without moving. The curtains did not fit the windows. At intervals the glare of a security light shone through the gap. He stretched out his arm to find the remote control and knocked the full ashtray off the arm of the chair.

The term 'omniscient' was introduced in Module 2 (page 88) to refer to the perspective of a narrator who knows the character well enough to make comments and judgements. The external view now involves the viewpoint of a human witness:

Cornelis is a busy man, he is always out and about. He has his warehouse to run, down in the harbour. At midday the Stock Market opens and he hurries down to the Bourse. Amsterdam is awash with capital and dealing there is brisk, often frenzied, because the place closes at two. In addition to this he has civic duties for he is a prominent citizen, a man of substance in this burgeoning city.

(*Tulip Fever*, by Deborah Moggach)

A 3rd-person narrative, 'he' or 'she', may be written from the perspective of one of the characters, describing the world through their eyes and with a flavour of their own words. This is called **internal narration**:

Lucy sat on the swing and pushed it as far back as her legs would allow. She lifted her feet off the ground and pulled herself into the seat. Lean *back* and push, lean *back* and push. She hadn't been able to swing herself at the beginning of the summer. Now she could swing herself far higher than Emma would push her. Lean back and push. She'd escaped from Emma. Emma would be *pissed off* – mum's favourite word. 'Wait in the playground,' Emma had said. She meant the small playground, but Lucy didn't want to do that. She liked the big playground better, even if it did mean a long walk.

(*Silent Playgrounds*, by Danuta Reah)

Narratives written in the 3rd person may shift between external and internal narration. The first two sentences of the extract from *Silent Playgrounds*, for example, are close to an outsider's view of the girl Lucy, before shifting into her perspective.

Stories can be told from a 1st-person perspective, 'I'. In these cases, the narrator will be one of the characters and offer the reader their point of view of the events. The style of narration will have a strong sense of the character's voice:

Chris was always faster than me going down Church Road hill. He had a BMX Sport series 3 which had smaller wheels and nifty riding position. Although this didn't change the speed any, it always looked as though he was travelling at 100 mph. My bike was far better on the straight, which was where I passed him, going through Drybeck Street and up into the Flats. I was the first kid in the street to get 16 gears, but more importantly, the first one to get professional curvy racer handlebars. They took a lot to get used to, putting more weight on your arms than on your arse, making your palms ache after long stretches, but it looked neat and gave you a little extra speed. I was way ahead when we left the Flats and crossed the road to Mire Pond. It was a blistering hot day, the first one we had all summer. The sky was almost white with sun, the heat making the tarmac on the road sticky to the touch as I bent down to check after I lay my bike on the pavement. Chris, like the show off he was, rode up to me with his shirt around his waist and his Raybans around his face.

Some narratives may even move between 3rd person and 1st person, but these shifts are usually signalled clearly, for example by a new chapter.

ACTIVITY 13

The following short story was written by a student to be read aloud in a school assembly. It deals with the problem of bullying. The target audience is 14–16-year-old pupils. The purpose is persuasive. Either read the story or listen to someone else reading it aloud.

- Remembering your own experience of school assemblies, how effective would this story be?

- Analyse the narrative structure, commenting on some of the following:

  - beginning / balance
  - middle / disharmony / problem / inciting moment
  - end / resolution.

- What perspective is used?

Now read the commentary on pages 174–175.

It was after Christmas. We'd just gone back to school. There was still snow on the ground. The pigeons used to slide their way to school. It made me laugh.

Tony wasn't at the same school as me. He stayed where he was when we moved. Mum and dad thought it would upset his education. It's their fault.

My dad doesn't live with us any more. I see him sometimes in the street and he gives me a hug and a kiss. I squirm, not because I don't like hugs and kisses, but because he doesn't feel like my dad anymore.

Tony and me used to watch TV late at night with the sound turned down so only we could hear it. Tony said he felt like a man on the moon. I told him I would love to be a spaceman. I didn't understand what he meant. It's my fault.

He told me all about being on the moon and the people there. He said it was a place as cold as you could ever imagine and all the people there are just dying to see you fall down. They push you and shove you and spit and kick you and you're there on your own. All your mates seem like they're a million miles away down there on earth. And your mum and dad are on the next planet after that. He said he couldn't speak to the people, because they didn't understand him, nobody understood him. He just had to stay there forever.

I caught my mum crying yesterday. She was holding a picture of Tony in the kitchen. Tony was smiling. I don't remember him like that. He did smile at me, but not that way, not for a long time. He smiled tight-lipped: his cheeks didn't seem to move, nor his eyes. It was as if there was something really important he had to do and couldn't for the life of him remember what it was. Maybe he was thinking about the moon.

I can remember saying 'Bye' to him, as we walked out of the front door. Tony slammed it shut. He walked one way and I walked the other.

I never saw him again. The police came round and asked me if I knew where he might have gone. I said, I knew where he wasn't.

Wherever he is, it's bound to be better than the moon. Whatever he's doing, he won't be having his face rubbed in dirt. He won't be punched until he can taste his blood, until he feels his bones ache and throb. He won't have to turn around every ten seconds to check there's no one there, check that he's not being followed. He won't be alone any more.

The reason why he went away was because his home, the place where he lived, became his own private prison cell. He was trapped. The no-win situation he was in became impossible to bear and, sooner or later, everyone became his enemy. He had to hate everyone, especially himself. His attackers demanded it.

He saw only one way out of this place he had been forced into and that was to run away as far as he could and never stop. Never stop running.

I look out of my window sometimes. It overlooks the world. I can see for miles. I look out and wonder what he's doing, out there in the great wide open, a million miles away from his moon.

I wonder if he would recognise me in the street; would I recognise him?

Wherever you are, whatever you're doing – Tony, the monsters are dead. So please come home. I miss you.

(Based on *Up on the Moon*, by Ali Gregory)

| ACTIVITY 14 | C3.1B | C3.3 | LP3.2 | WO3.2 | WO3.3 |

Write a short story (500–700 words) to be read aloud in school assembly.

- Choose an appropriate topic for either 11–13 or 14–16-year-olds.

- Make an outline of the elements of the story. Decide on the perspective of the narrative.

- In small groups, read the stories aloud and offer constructive criticism. Comment on the development of the plot, and the choice of perspective.

- Choose one story to present to the full group. Make any necessary changes.

- If possible, read the story aloud and get feedback from the target age group.

No commentary.

Activity 14 set the writing task for you, but there are many other possibilities, if you decide to produce a short story for your folder. The story can be aimed at readers, rather than listeners; it can be for a different audience; the purpose can be to entertain.

It is essential to write about what you know, or, at least, what you are able to imagine in convincing detail, so beware of choosing characters and events that are completely outside your experience.

Writing a short story can be a very rewarding experience, but do not underestimate the challenge. There are many specialist books and courses on the writing of literary forms such as short stories, drama and poetry.

Writing for readers

Feature articles

This section covers various types of feature articles. These are different from news stories, which require access to facts that the student writer would rarely have. For this reason such a task is not usually suitable for a student writer. Personal columns rely on the intrinsic interest of a famous name, so are not feasible tasks for an unknown writer either.

Style and approach of feature articles

What distinguishes feature articles from a discursive essay, a narrative or a personal account? Unlike other forms of writing, a newspaper or magazine is not read from cover to cover or out of necessity. Journalism is generally read as a leisure activity and is browsed through. News stories may be skimmed for information, but, once a feature article has been chosen, it is read *intensively* for pleasure. Peter Morris, a journalist, has offered this analogy: 'If news writing is marching up and down in strict order and writing personal columns is partying, then feature writing is strolling purposefully down the street wanting to know when the party started and why.' This allows a range of approaches and styles, but you should avoid straying into other genres such as discursive essay, narrative or personal account.

The first task of the feature writer is to attract the reader's attention. This needs to be done in the opening lines (the headline is normally written by the sub-editor). The same journalist gives this advice: 'Feature writers use a variety of techniques from the sensational to the sly, teasing or intriguing opening.' Collect examples of openings to feature articles and see how they attract your attention. Some examples are provided in Activity 15.

Once you have hooked your reader with your opening sentence, you have to keep them interested. This is where the quality of writing comes into its own. Journalism borrows freely from other areas such as poetry, advertising, humour and rhetoric in its use of techniques that delight the human ear or mind. You will notice the use of questions, alliteration, exaggeration and innovative phrasing. But these do not guarantee success. Alliteration and rhetorical questions can be overdone. Find journalistic articles that impress you and note the techniques used. Two examples are provided in Activity 19.

The term 'eye candy' is a criticism sometimes levelled at the style of journalism in general. This suggests a superficial attraction. To counteract this potential triviality, the writer needs also to provide a sound argument.

Here then, are the three points in summary:

1 provoke interest

2 use lively style

3 give evidence.

Provoke interest

ACTIVITY 15

The following openings have been taken from the work of both students and professional journalists. Read through these openings as if you were browsing through a newspaper or magazine.

- Rank them according to their appeal to you as a reader. Also note those that you think would appeal to a different group of readers (e.g. age or interest).

- Comment on the ways in which the openings provoke interest.

Now read the commentary on pages 175–176.

1   Part-time work! Even the sound of this makes my toes curl. It cannot be forgotten though that part-time work is a necessity for many, and has an important role to play in creating a streamlined society.

2   Welcome my friends to another heated debate on 'Popular Culture'. If you have been following the series you will have noticed that Mr Adorno and ourselves have been battling it out with our pens at the ready.

3   **Golf – Let's putt it into perspective.** We all know someone who is afflicted by the golfing bug. Maybe it's the next-door neighbour or someone at work who religiously plays every Friday afternoon, but have you ever wondered what all the fuss is about?

4   Nightclubs have become something of an institution in themselves. They are found in every town and city and are the most popular choice of entertainment when going out on a Friday or Saturday night.

5   America was first. Britain is next. The release of the new *Star Wars* film has had adults and children alike clutching at their light sabres and worshipping their Jedi figures with a reverence that was last seen when the Beatles conquered the galaxy.

6   This week *Overrated* is looking at arguably the most dominating sport in the world. Not only is it a sport, but it is a multi-million pound industry that's growing in stature every 90 minutes.

7   It can be said that Britain really has gone soap crazy. Not only are we tuning in to watch the number on offer, but we're buying magazines, posters, T-shirts, mugs and other nick nacks to do with our favourite programmes.

8   **The Old World re-ordered**. I'm tired, my stomach is making water buffalo mating calls and I'm finding it hard to see. But, I'm still playing Final Fantasy VII. Is it good? Merely good? No. Should it be made a compulsory part of the National Curriculum? Maybe. Am I losing sleep, food, and quite possibly friends over it? Unfortunately, yes.

9   Walking around a mucky path lit with buzzing glowflies, our host warns us about how strong the smoke is out here. 'Knocks you right out,' he says, 'you won't be able to move your legs for hours.' Heard it all before, mate. Apparently the two Argentinean girls in the hut across the path have got some on the burn. So we pop round with the obligatory bottle of the excellent Bacardi spice, seeing as we've been given six bottles of the stuff to take with us, and sure enough there's an ultra spliff with wings waiting to kill us.

10 Though TSR have finally gone belly up, AD&D still thrives and so Interplay have decided to finally put the Forgotten Realms licence they acquired many moons ago to good use.

ACTIVITY 16   WO3.2   WO3.3

The task is to write a feature article for the series *Overrated* which aims to persuade readers that an aspect of popular culture (sport, TV, music, etc.) is overrated.

- Choose a topic for this task and write the opening sentences *only*.

- Comment on the techniques you have used to provoke interest.

- Give constructive criticism on other students' opening sentences.

No commentary.

Colloquial style

A modern journalistic article does not use the dry, impersonal style of an essay. Most writers adopt a more colloquial style, as in this article by Shane Watson in the *Guardian*.

> [Dr Raj Persaud] also found that 'women increase their vocabulary complexity when men join their group'. This would be great news if you believed a word of it. Arabella Weir's Fast Show character – the capable career girl who goes all googly helpless dolly whenever men are around – did not get air time on account of being a quaint anachronism but because she is a fact of life.

There is an interesting mixture of styles in this short extract. Watson follows the formality of the quotation with a comment in a more colloquial style: 'great news if you believed a word of it'. She uses slang: 'googly helpless dolly', jargon: 'air time' and more elevated vocabulary: 'quaint anachronism' in one sentence. This long sentence with a comment in parenthesis follows the shorter dismissive comment.

The advantage of using colloquial features lies in the creation of a direct, conversational tone.

However, some chatty, personal styles of language are not effective on the written page (see page 133). The following list suggests features of colloquial language:

- 1st-person pronouns 'I', 'me', including the audience with 'we', 'us'

- direct address to the audience with 2nd-person pronouns 'you'

- long, loosely structured sentences

- fillers such as 'well', 'now', 'anyway' to introduce statements

- added comments in parenthesis (brackets or commas)

- added adverbs, such as 'really', 'surely', 'actually'

- interrogatives and imperatives.

ACTIVITY 17

The following two extracts use features of colloquial language, but these sometimes lack impact.

- Identify colloquial features and comment on their effectiveness.

Now read the commentary on pages 176–177.

EXTRACT 1

Soaps aren't all bad really and you probably wouldn't think it but I watch a few on occasions. However, as I believe it is fine to watch one or two soaps (avoid Australian and American ones!) every now and again, don't rework your lives to fit around the soaps and avoid omnibuses at all costs. You could be leading a much more productive life in your spare time. Soaps are overrated in my opinion and they are taken far too seriously ...

Then again, can eighteen million people really be so wrong? It doesn't really matter how much this article states that soap operas are overrated, millions will still watch the soaps, buy the T-shirts ...

EXTRACT 2

Women kick back

Fed up of being second best, me too. I mean alright once, twice even three times but when every Saturday for ten months you come second best to a blow-up ball it can get a bit tedious. Football has and looks like continuing to be the country's number one sport taking over many of the old traditional cultures, but surely women are more important than the game and after suffering in silence for long enough it's about time that we women got together and did something. It's about time we realised that we don't have to put up with this, what have we done to deserve it – nothing, so join with me in saying *no* to footie.

What's the kick?

It has often puzzled me to see my husband sat there, shouting at the television screen. Why? Because in reality all that's happening is a ball is being kicked between men in an attempt to put it in the net. Now why is it men become so involved, and why is it women put up with it?

What do we want?

British life wouldn't be the same without football. There would be no hooliganism at football matches, there would be no bullying for the team you support, there would be no footballers being paid thirty thousand a week. That's not an attempt to put you off football because it is too late. All we want is to be acknowledged. *Don't* put us second best when we want to be first, *don't* cry over a game that the players get well paid for and *do* involve us. Women like the game, if only for the legs we see.

So men – enough of the crying, enough of the shouting – there is more to life.

And women – enough of the crying, enough of the shouting, join me and Let's *Kick Back!*

ACTIVITY 18 | PS3.3

Re-draft Extract 2 in Activity 17, so that it keeps the lively, direct tone, but is clearer for a reader.

- Note the changes made. (These would be referred to in a commentary on your own writing.)

No commentary.

Rhetorical features

The study of rhetoric identifies devices used in speeches to sway the emotions of the listeners. Such devices are also used in writing, particularly in writing to persuade. However, reading a text is a more distant and leisurely activity than being present at a speech delivered to a crowd, so the devices need to be used with some restraint. Some of the common devices are listed below (taken from *Original Writing*, by Alison Ross).

Emotional appeals

- Asking opinion of listener / reader
- Offering oneself as surety
- Complimenting the audience
- Threatening disaster
- Disparaging the opinion of opponents
- Mocking opposing views by exaggeration
- Using an emotional exclamation
- Exhorting the audience to action
- Summarising in an impassioned manner.

Stylistic techniques

- Metaphor and simile
- Alliteration
- Balanced phrases / use of opposites in balanced phrases
- Listing (often in threes) and building up to a climax
- Repetition
- Emotive words.

ACTIVITY 19 C3.1A

Read the following extracts from two feature articles. One is written by a student and the other by a professional journalist.

- Can you tell which is which?

- Comment on the rhetorical devices used.

    - What emotional appeals are made to the readers and how effective do you find them?
    - What stylistic techniques are used and how effective do you find them?
    - Indicate any phrases that you feel are overdone.

Now read the commentary on page 177.

EXTRACT 1

The Millennium pile of old cobblers!

Is it me or recently have people been going mad for the millennium? The idea of stocking up food months in advance because of this farcical celebration is beyond me. Don't get me wrong, I will probably be part of the rat race to get food leading up to the millennium. I'll be there in Tesco's with the rest of you scratching and clawing away trying to get enough food to nibble on leading up to the big event.

But is there really any point in this over-hyped occasion? Is it not just another day? What are we celebrating anyway, the 2000th birthday of Christ? Hold on a minute, doesn't he have a birthday every year? I wonder what percentage of people who will be celebrating are actually Christians, and whether Mr Christ will be in the forefront of their minds as the clock strikes twelve and we all fall down, as it were.

[...]

The biggest travesty surrounding this whole joke of a celebration is the ridiculous amount of money spent by our government on celebrating this monumentous event. Millions of pounds. Could it have been spent on education? ('I lost an eye due to staff incompetence and undermanning but I had a great millennium!'). Millions of pounds that could have been used for charities, the homeless (bet they will have a great day and Kosovan refugees – so will they.) Millions of pounds that could have been invaluable for countless parts of our society, but what do they decide to do instead? Build a dome. Ah, but it's a millennium dome, a symbol of British achievement in the twentieth century. A great huge white nipple that cost millions won't be ready on time and to top it all off they're selling it to the Chinese.

[...]

I'll tell you where I'll be, I'll be tucked up in bed fast asleep sound in the knowledge that I'll probably be the only one in the western world (who wasn't working) without a hangover, ready to start the new millennium afresh.

EXTRACT 2

There is something hideously unsexy about busy, efficient or 'driven' people. As for 'thrusting', as used in the context of work, well, what are they trying to overcompensate for? (Just think of poor Ian Beale in *Eastenders*.) Imagine how bad in bed those men who are always in a hurry must be; those mobile drones with their phones on the train, wanting everything done last week.

And the sort of strange woman who finds such men attractive! They obviously looked a bit too long at Adam Chance in *Crossroads* and never got over it. Chances are that, if you *are* 'busy, busy, busy' (and, obviously, I'm talking here about white-collar workers, not nurses or people looking after their old parents), you are actually thick, thick, thick, because you haven't got the wit to skive, skive, skive or delegate, delegate, delegate.

Busy people often act like martyrs, but the fact is that they are tremendous egoists; they believe – or at least they want the onlooker to believe – that if they let up for one minute the world will end. I don't for a moment believe that about myself or anybody, and indeed the fact is that most people would do their jobs better if they did them less, not more. Don't make that deadline; take the long way home. When you see two queues, stand in the longer one and daydream. And look, Chicken Licken, the sky still won't fall down.

ACTIVITY 20   C3.3   LP3.2   IT3.3

Write the full article from the opening sentence you wrote in Activity 16. Give yourself a limited time to complete it – no more than two hours.

- In groups, offer constructive criticism as in Activity 16.

- Re-draft the article in the light of the feedback.

- If you have access to a word-processing package, use visuals to enhance your text. This would be necessary for a locally produced magazine. Remember, though, that this is not the job of a professional journalist, who would submit only the text for the production team to work on.

No commentary.

Using presentation devices

This section groups together several genres because they share the element of visual presentation devices. These include leaflets, pamphlets and booklets, terms which are not clearly differentiated, but which all involve a number of pages collated together. Information packs and fact files may be a collection of single sheets. Posters and adverts are single-sided; display boards can be two-sided. Magazine feature articles also use layout features.

You should collect examples of texts that use presentation devices before doing the activities in this section. It is important to supply 'style models' in your folder, if you are submitting a text in a particular genre. Once you are aware of the conventions, you can refer to these to explain the choices and decisions you made when re-drafting your text.

ACTIVITY 21

Use the texts you have collected which provide examples of types of presentation devices, and complete this table for each one, noting which devices are used. 'White space' refers to blank space between text, pictures, etc.

Visual device	Name of text
Pictures, logos, etc.	
Graphs, tables, diagrams	
Flow charts	
Boxed summaries	
Headings	
Short paragraphs	
Columns	
White space	
Lists with numbers or bullet points	
Colours	
Different print sizes and font (types)	
Capitals, bold and italic print	
Highlighted quotes	
Other	

No commentary.

Style of text

This section will examine the effective use of devices such as headings and lists to enhance the text. The text itself, however, is fundamental and cannot be rescued by visuals, however attractive. The purpose of such texts is often to inform, instruct or advise, in which case the style needs to be as clear as possible. Some leaflets and flyers are produced with a persuasive purpose, so may adopt a more rhetorical style. For Activity 22, choose a text with an informative or advisory purpose.

ACTIVITY 22   WO3.1   WO3.2

Work in groups to study the text of your chosen leaflet. Focus on sentence structure, vocabulary and tone.

- Sentence structure. Which of the four sentence types are used?

    - statements
    - interrogatives
    - imperatives
    - exclamations.

    Which are used for headings and which for main text?
    Are the sentences mainly:

    - simple
    - compound (linked with 'and', 'but', 'or')
    - complex (clauses linked by subordinating conjunctions, such as 'if', 'which', 'that', 'although', or by subordinate verbs ending in '-ing' or '-ed').

- Vocabulary. What do you notice about the type and level of vocabulary used? Are there any idioms, images, slang, technical terms or jargon?

- Tone. How would you describe the tone used – personal / impersonal, colloquial / formal, etc.? What personal pronouns are used?

No commentary.

You will use the analysis from Activities 21 and 22 for Activity 23, which asks you to make some constructive criticism of first drafts of leaflets. Your comments should refer, not only to the use of presentation devices, but to the effectiveness of their style.

Use and style of headings and lists

Leaflets can be read in a different way from continuous prose. As leaflets often have an informative purpose, it is not necessary to read every word. The text can be skimmed for gist or scanned for specific information. Clear headings allow the reader to do this more effectively.

Headings should give a brief indication of the topic of the section that follows. They can often be phrased as questions to provide a sense of interaction between the reader and the text. Other devices can be used to make them lively and eye-catching, such as alliteration, puns or allusions to well-known sayings. Such features should be used with caution, as a self-consciously witty tone may irritate the readers.

Lists, often numbered or marked with bullet points, are very useful to indicate a series of brief, related points. Remember:

- the theme, or topic, of the list must be indicated in the introductory sentence

- the points must be phrased concisely

- the order should be logical

- the points should all have a similar structure.

ACTIVITY 23 — WO3.1 — WO3.2 — WO3.3

Extract 1 gives the opening, topic headings and closing section of a leaflet, giving advice on preparing for interviews.

Extract 2 gives an example of a list with bullet points.

Read each extract, discuss them in groups and revise a section each.

- Comment on the tone of the opening and closing sections.

- How effective are the headings?

- How effective are the lists in extracts 1 and 2?

- Re-draft the outline extract, making any changes you feel are necessary to the tone, headings and lists.

- Review the changes that each member of the group has made.

Now read the commentary on page 177.

EXTRACT 1

STARTING OFF

Your first step into preparing for an interview is to stay calm! You will not be any use to yourself or the interviewers if you panic! Take deep breaths and try not to worry.

Throughout your life you will have many hurdles in your way, all you have to do is jump over them. As soon as you have jumped one, the rest will get easier.

QUESTIONS
HOW TO PREPARE YOUR OWN QUESTIONS
PUNCTUALITY
MAKE SURE OF WHERE YOU ARE GOING
APPEARANCE
SPEAKING

Here are some main pointers for you to remember.

1. STAY CALM!!

2. Prepare some questions you may want to ask.

3. Have some idea of the kinds of questions they will ask you!

4. Be on time!

5. Make sure you know where you're going!

6. Look smart!
Act smart!
Be smart!

7. If you are really worried about your interview, get a teacher, parent or friend to help you act out how you think your interview will go. Prepare yourself for the formality of sitting in a room with people asking you questions. Prepare yourself to answer some likely questions.

Ask your teacher or parents what interviews can be like for courses at university and job interviews. If anyone knows, they do!

And last of all, remember, it will not be as bad as you think it will be!

FURTHER READING – write to ...

EXTRACT 2

The Big Day ...

- Well, now that the big day has arrived, all of our preparations can be put into practice.

- Have a good breakfast. Something that will fill you up without giving you indigestion.

- How about cereal, toast and a hot drink? Tea or coffee perhaps.

- Give yourself plenty of time to get ready, *don't* rush yourself.

- Avoid trying a 'new look', it is best to stick with what's familiar to you as far as hair, make-up, etc. is concerned.

- When you set off for the interview remember to take with you:

 – any notes you have made about questions to ask or courses relevant
 – a pen and paper for any last minute thoughts
 – some money in case you need a drink or something such as spare tights
 – an umbrella if it looks like it may rain.

- Try to relax, don't worry about the interview. Just be yourself and present yourself in a manner you are familiar with.

ACTIVITY 24   C3.3   IT3.1   IT3.2   IT3.3

Produce a leaflet, fact sheet or handout giving information or advice on a topic you are familiar with.

- Decide on your target audience and where the text will be distributed.

- You may need to find more information, using the internet or other sources.

- Get feedback from the intended readers of your text and re-draft it.

- If you have access to a word-processing package, use visuals to enhance the presentation.

No commentary.

Writing a commentary

A student chose as his task to write a review of a computer game. The task is individual, feasible and appropriately demanding. The review below was written for readers of a computer game magazine, so the primary purpose is to persuade, but the writing also gives information. The game is one that the student recently acquired and the magazines are ones that he regularly reads. The student's commentary is discussed in Activity 26.

Arachnophobia hits the little grey box

Anyone who at any time has had the slightest wave of terror when confronted by an eight legged intruder in their bath need read no further. Software guru BMG's new platformer, spider, has arrived. It's crawling with more insects than you could possibly imagine. Not just spiders, there are bats, grasshoppers, wasps and a host of other annoyances to thwart your journey.

Years of Nanotechnology have allowed mankind to produce spiders with weapon implants. This allows the tiny blighters to wander around undetected, while following the proverbial bad guys, as they make good their escape from the labs where this particular spider was developed.

This will take you through streets, labs, museums, sewers and a factory. Each level has sub-stages and you must locate all the micro chips which are in effect all exits from the levels. This unlocks other areas in the game and allows you to progress. Otherwise you need to go back on yourself to locate them and clear the way ahead.

The potential for a fully interactive 3D world is phenomenal but unfortunately we're offered a predetermined path and cannot stray from it at any time. This restricts the player enormously and most of the time the enjoyment factor also.

Picture a game similar to *Pandemonium* in that, while the rendered backgrounds and pretty 3D foregrounds are very nice, the path is rigidly set so that you can only go over obstacles rather than round them. When was the last time you saw a spider run in a set direction without once changing its course to avoid an obstacle?

You need also to adapt to the initially strange spider control as to which direction you are heading. If, for example, you are moving right and then have to move up a wall, you will have to press up to make the spider climb the wall. In other words, every time the spider heads in a new direction, you must press the corresponding direction otherwise you'll be left stranded. It sounds simple, and it is, but it does take a little getting used to when you first play.

The spiders themselves do actually move realistically and are as creepy and disgusting as you'd expect. The eight legged furry beasts have never looked so good, or bad, depending on your point of view. You can cling to surfaces anywhere, although touching things such as fans or electrical wires can render you an ex-spider. Other than this you can safely wander underneath crates or girders. As stated earlier, though, the path is so rigidly set out you can't really go far wrong – if you can't head in a certain direction the spider simply won't go.

As is the case with *Pandemonium* and the like, you can pick up 100 icons for an extra life. These are allegedly DNA strands and are dotted around the levels. Depending on how confident you are, you can either collect these or ignore them and head straight for your mission objectives. If you're in a hurry you may wish to ignore them, but it's not too difficult to collect them on your way. It does become tiresome trying to pick up all the icons you come across as it's a stop / start affair as you jump to collect the higher ones and check under every block, conveyor belt or ledge.

The spider itself is far from being a real tough character; two hits from any foe will prove fatal. To counter this, there are health capsules throughout the stages and you must find these if you are to survive. Then you can live to fight another battle and another and another ad infinitum, without too much of a worry.

In general this game is a satisfying romp through the world from a spider's point of view and, if you ignore its short lifespan, will provide you with a few hours of entertainment.

Half of the marks for your coursework folder are awarded for the commentary and the awareness you show of the writing and re-drafting process. You may write a single commentary comparing the texts for an audience of listeners, rather than one of readers. You may prefer to write two separate commentaries on each text. The total word length should not be much more than 1500 words, excluding quotations.

What is the difference between a commentary on your own writing and an analysis of texts such as the ones you studied in Module 1 and Module 2? Both require awareness of the ways that language features create stylistic effects, but the approach and emphasis is different.

A stylistic analysis of a text looks at the text from the point of view of the *reader*. This means that the process of creating the text is not known. Close attention to the style should reveal the writer's purpose, intended audience and the genre.

The task of the commentary is to illuminate the *process* of creating a written text from the point of view of the *writer*. Connections are made between the style of the text and its purpose, target audience and genre.

First, what not to do in a commentary:

- Avoid making vague, general claims about the style, for example 'I used a friendly tone / formal style / semi-informal style / a mixture of formal and informal vocabulary.' Try to be more specific about the tone and always provide an example from your text.

- Avoid quoting from your text without identifying what, precisely, is significant about your quote, for example 'I tried not to sound too self-congratulatory: "I hit a screamer into the top corner, which I am still reliving today!"' Explain that you were mocking yourself by the exaggerated reaction – 'still reliving today'.

- Avoid making 'negative points', for example 'I didn't use any jargon / slang / complex sentences / metaphors, etc.' Say what you did use.

- Don't make illogical connections between a feature of the text and its supposed effect on the reader, for example 'I used alliteration (or colloquial vocabulary, short sentences, bullet points, etc.) to make the text flow / create a friendly relationship with the reader / make it interesting, etc.' Think realistically about the effect of such features.

- Don't paraphrase (summarise) your text, for example 'First I gave an account of ... And then I went on to describe ...' It's not necessary to explain this to the reader; explain stylistic choices instead.

- Do not 'feature-spot', however impressive the terminology, for example 'I used proper nouns / anaphoric and cataphoric reference / free morphemes, etc.' Only mention relevant features.

This final point is, perhaps, the hardest to avoid. It is understandable that the writer of the commentary wants to display their awareness of linguistic terminology. It is tricky to learn all the terms and then show judgement about which are significant to this particular task.

So, how should you approach the commentary?

A commentary is awarded marks for a thoughtful discussion of relevant and significant features of the text. When deciding what is relevant and significant, you need to bear in mind:

- the purpose of your text

- the intended audience

- the genre.

For marks in the higher bands, you need to be able to go further than a discussion of content, graphology and vocabulary. While this may involve discussing features of grammar, you are advised to begin with the larger issues of overall structure and discourse. This will lead you into analysis of the relevant features of grammar and vocabulary. The terms 'Overall structure' and 'discourse' are explained below and exemplified in Activity 25.

Overall structure

When you analyse the overall structure of a text (either spoken or written), look first at the way it opens and closes. The genre often dictates how you begin and end a text. The conventions are more prescribed for some genres, while others leave more scope for creativity. Fairy stories and folk tales have more predictable openings and closings than short stories, for example: 'Once upon a time, there was ...', '... and they lived happily ever after.' You looked at some characteristic features of openings to feature articles, but they may capture interest by *suggesting* other genres. Openings to talks usually both greet the audience and introduce the topic; openings to leaflets usually concentrate on the topic.

ACTIVITY 25

Identify the context for the following openings and closings.

- We are gathered here together ...

- Dear Occupier, Congratulations! You have won ...

- Hallo, Franklin Travel. Can I help you?

- It was a dark and stormy night and the brigands were there ...

- Thank you! You've been a wonderful audience. Goodnight.

- CYL8R Jonny.

- Will Angel have the courage to tell her? Tune in next week to find out.

- Are you sure you want to log off?

In your commentary, discuss the way you have opened and closed your text. Did you have much of a choice? What influenced your decision?

No commentary.

Discourse

The term 'discourse' is used here to refer to the relationship adopted between the writer of the text and the audience. You can begin by thinking about the relative status of writer and audience. Do you address them as equals, as if they are known to you, or in more impersonal way? Do you create some authority or distance? Are you friendly or confrontational? Then think about the features of your text that created the discourse relationship. It is always worth looking at pronoun use and colloquial features, but it is impossible to have a checklist. Try to look at your text afresh and begin with intuitive judgements about significant features. Once you have highlighted these, describe them using the correct terminology.

ACTIVITY 26

Read the following commentary on the text 'Arachnophobia hits the little grey box' on pages 160–161. The writer explains how the style of the text achieves the desired purpose, audience relationship and genre.

- Indicate the points made on the following aspects of language use:

    - discourse: writer–reader / listener relationship; tone of voice
    - overall structure: openings, closings and links
    - grammar: sentence types – interrogatives and imperatives (modal verbs); sentence structure – minor and simple; pronoun use
    - vocabulary: colloquial, slang, formal, technical, jargon, etc.
    - graphology and layout: use of presentation devices
    - content: choice and balance of detail.

Now read the commentary on page 178.

Commentary on computer game review

I chose this task as I am a Playstation enthusiast and regularly read reviews of the latest games in specialist games magazines. I enjoy the style of such journalism, as it seems to be speaking in *my* language – modern, colloquial, witty and intelligent (*sample enclosed*). I imagine that the typical writer is young, male and educated writing for young males addicted by computer games. Reviews have a dual purpose – to provide detailed information about the game and to offer an opinion about its worth. The style of it should also be enjoyable to read. My aim was to achieve all three in my review. The style is, I hope, a dynamic mixture of the colloquial and the formal / technical.

Colloquial features establish the impression of personal interaction between writer and reader – we buy such magazines to enjoy being part of this sub-group. The reader is addressed directly as 'you', sometimes with questions and imperatives: 'Picture a game ...', 'When was the last time you saw a spider ...?' I use phrases from everyday spoken language, such as 'getting used to', as well as more obvious features of slang: 'creepy' and some non-standard forms: 'real tough'. Such vocabulary is important to indicate youth and non-conformity to 'correct, formal' English.

Computer jargon is there, showing that the audience share detailed knowledge of this world. Some phrases are commonplace: 'a fully interactive 3D world', but others are more exclusive: 'Software guru BMG's new platformer' and 'Years of Nanotechnology'. General scientific vocabulary is assumed to be familiar also: 'DNA strands'. There is always a problem of image for computer enthusiasts, so it is important to have some lighter, humorous touches, to show that we are not all anti-social geeks. The fact that this game involves spiders shows the game-makers themselves are aware of the need not to be too serious. Many references to the spiders in the text keeps it light and down-to-earth, but I also played with various, clichéd synonyms: 'eight legged furry beasts'.

Computer games may be thought of as the domain of urban, unemployed youth. This stereotype is contested by the articulate style of the magazines. There are phrases which would not be out of place for an Oxford don in the following paragraph for example:

The spider itself is far from being [...]
Two hits from any foe will prove fatal.
To counter this [...] if you are to survive.
Then you can live to fight another battle [...] ad infinitum

There is the use of archaic vocabulary such as 'foe', the Latin phrase 'ad infinitum' and the formality of the verb phrases: 'is far from being ... if you are to survive'. However, to avoid an over-formal impression, they are 'cut-away' with colloquialisms like 'real tough'. This gives a tongue in cheek attitude – we can do the posh stuff, if we want to. This mixture of colloquial and formal is a feature of modern media – the stylistic equivalent of Estuary English or wearing a sharp suit with a skimpy T-shirt.

The genre of journalism also requires a particular approach and structure. The opening sentence must serve as a 'hook' to get the browsing reader to continue. This can be done in various ways to intrigue, shock or involve the reader. For my hook opening, I chose to use the sort of warning that always has the opposite effect, like 'Viewers of a nervous disposition are warned not to watch this.' I also used the sort of description that excludes no one, like a Jehovah's Witness asking, 'Do you care about the state of the world?' Nearly everyone has an aversion to spiders, yet they will disregard the warning and read on. As well as using the variety of registers analysed above, I use a variety of sentence lengths and structures to maintain interest. Because of the nature of the topic, sentences often need to be complex, but I was careful to keep the occasional sentence short and simple for contrast: 'Other than this you can safely wander underneath crates and girders.' If anything, I would use more short sentences another time. The review ends predictably with a summarising assessment of the game; in words it is described fairly positively as 'a satisfying romp [...] a few hours of entertainment.' The numerical assessment is in line with the habit to assign scores as a more succinct evaluation.

[720 words including quotes]

Putting the folder together

Choosing appropriate tasks

Your folder should contain two pieces of writing that demonstrate your versatility as a writer. There are two 'must-do' requirements for your choice of task:

1. The tasks must be differentiated in their purpose. You should choose two of the following purposes:

   - entertain

   - persuade

   - inform

   - instruct / advise.

2. The tasks must be differentiated in mode:

   - one task must be in a spoken mode, i.e. for a listening audience
   - the other must be in a written mode, i.e. for a reading audience.

   Here are some other points to bear in mind:

   - If you aim your work at different audiences (rather than both for teenagers, for example), you are more likely to use a clearly distinct style for each.

   - It is not so important to vary the topic, if you have a particular interest in, say, sport or music.

   - Each task should be individual, feasible and appropriately demanding. Each of these criteria is discussed in the following sections.

Individual tasks

Although you will do some set writing exercises in class, it is not a good idea for each person to submit the same task in the folder of coursework. Each person's skills and interests will differ, so you should choose a task that suits you.

One way to decide is to imagine the types of writing that teachers and examiners might value. This was probably the case with a student who wrote a description of a walk in a valley. Sights and sounds were described in detail, but it failed to engage the interest of the reader – the phrasing was rather predictable and therefore unconvincing. When questioned further, the student explained that she wasn't writing about a particular walk or valley; in fact she didn't go for walks in valleys and didn't have any desire to do so. She just thought that descriptions of nature were the right sort of thing to write about. A much more successful venture into writing was the student who wrote about a rock concert he had recently been to. He thought the band was great and decided to write a review, using the style of music reviews in *NME* (*New Musical Express*) as his model.

You do not have to write to someone else's agenda in coursework. This is your chance to choose the tasks that best fit your interests, knowledge and skills. Don't worry if you haven't got easily labelled hobbies, like stamp collecting or Kung Fu. Think about how you choose to spend time. Even sleeping. Eddie Izzard didn't get out of bed for a year. It may have seemed like a complete waste of time, but it gave him lots of bizarre material. Joanne Harris used her passion for chocolate in her novel *Chocolat*.

ACTIVITY 27 | C3.1A

- Choose two of the following and make notes:

  - Time capsule – pick ten objects that leave an impression of your life and personality.
  - List five memorable occasions.
  - What would the perfect week's break involve?
  - List your pet hates – if you could make some things disappear with the wave of a magic wand, what would they be? Be specific, for example talk about *Brookside* rather than 'Poverty'.

- Compare in small groups. This may bring up ideas to add to your list.

- Now think specifically about your taste in language. Make a list in two columns.

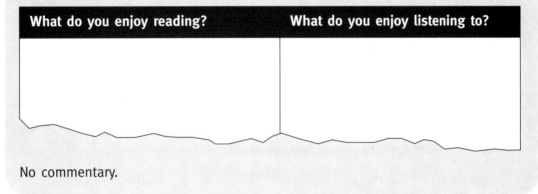

What do you enjoy reading?	What do you enjoy listening to?

No commentary.

Feasible tasks

The task you choose should be one that would have a purpose and audience outside the classroom. There are many examples of exercises that are useful as practice for various writing skills, but which do not fulfil any real purpose. Perhaps the days of being set 'A Day in the Life of a Penny' are over, but the following are common: a tabloid newspaper report of the Battle of Hastings; a live radio broadcast of the shooting of President Kennedy; a holiday brochure for trips to the moon. Each exercise is a useful way of understanding the differences between genres – tabloid journalism, spontaneous news reports, advertising brochures. However, because these tasks do not have any real purpose and audience, they would be difficult to criticise and re-draft in a meaningful way. A live radio broadcast is, by definition, not scripted so it can't be changed or improved. If the text was criticised for being muddled or over-emotional, the writer might maintain, 'Well, that's what they would have said.'

If you are writing a pastiche (imitation or parody) of a particular genre, it is sometimes possible to redefine the task in terms of purpose and audience. A newspaper report usually has an informative purpose, but writing in the style of a newspaper about a fictional or historical event might be done to entertain readers of feature pages, or even to persuade an editor that you could replicate the house style. Whether it would be effective for either of these purposes is another question.

ACTIVITY 28 — PS3.1

Here are some examples of tasks that have problems regarding feasibility. These problems become clear if you ask the following questions:

- Where might it be broadcast or published?
- Who would read it or listen to it?
- What is the intended purpose of the text?
- How might the writer re-draft it to make it more effective for the purpose or audience?

1 An interview with an imaginary Aids sufferer.
2 A step-by-step 'Learn to Swim' booklet.
3 A magazine article about the death of Marilyn Monroe.
4 William Hague's keynote speech for the Conservative Party Conference.
5 An advertisement for the biggest transistor in the world.
6 The history of poetry.
7 A speech on the legalisation of cannabis.
8 'How to Play the Guitar' manual.
9 A dialogue between Shakespeare's Iago and Milton's Satan.
10 The opening chapter of a novel.
11 A leaflet on homelessness – to be delivered door-to-door.
12 A Manchester City match programme.

Make a table like the one below and fill it in for the twelve tasks listed:

	1	2	3	4	5	6	7	8	9	10	11	12
Can't be done by a student												
Can't be done by anyone												
Already done												
Pointless – who would want to read / listen to it?												
Wouldn't work												
Impossible to say whether it would work												
A feasible task for a student writer												

No commentary.

Appropriately demanding tasks

Some tasks simply do not require advanced writing skills. These are tasks where the text follows an easily replicated formula, often the same simple structures repeated over and over again. These usually occur in the inform and instruct categories. The following tasks are not appropriately demanding:

- a recipe / menu

- a knitting / dressmaking pattern

- the rules for a board game

- a gardening catalogue

- a guide to city-centre clothes shops

- a diary.

There is also a problem with children's stories that rely mainly on pictures for their appeal, for example 'Harry Hedgehog and his family have a happy day at the seaside and come home again.' However, you could write a story to be read aloud to young children, with a plot that would entertain both adults and children.

A good way to assess the level of the task is to notice whether you encountered problems writing the first draft and struggled to make effective changes in successive drafts. If it seemed straightforward the first time round and you didn't need to make any significant changes, the task was probably not demanding enough.

ACTIVITY 29   LP3.1   LP3.2

- Choose two tasks for your coursework folder, following the guidelines above.

- Note the primary purpose, audience and genre. Estimate the word length, if possible.

- Seek feedback on your choice of tasks:

  - Are they differentiated in terms of listening v. reading audience and primary purpose?
  - Do they suit your interests and knowledge?
  - Would they have a real purpose and audience outside the classroom?
  - Will you be able to demonstrate a range of writing skills?

No commentary.

Organising your coursework folder

The first page of your coursework folder will be the candidate record form. This will provide a brief summary of the two pieces and commentary / commentaries.

You can include your own table of contents, if you wish. Then arrange the folder, so that the teacher and moderator can easily locate the pieces for assessment. It may help to use coloured dividers. For each of the two texts, place the final draft first, followed by the commentary. After this, include evidence of drafting and any source material or bibliographies. If you have written a single commentary, place this after the material for each of the two texts.

Your folder should contain material in this order:

- candidate record form

- final draft of text 1

- commentary for text 1 (if there are separate commentaries)

- drafts for text 1

- source material or bibliography for text 1

- final draft of text 2

- commentary for text 2 (or commentary on both texts)

- drafts for text 2

- source material or bibliography for text 2.

Thinking ahead to Module 4

There is a coursework module in the A2 course that also involves your own writing. 'Text Transformation' requires you to take a literary work of any genre – prose, drama or poetry – and transform the work into another genre. This transformation may involve a different audience or purpose. There are examples of possible tasks in the 'Specification for the Language and Literature' course.

Your first task is to select a literary text, so it would be useful to consider this choice before you embark on the second year of the course. The text should be one that you know well and appreciate. It could be one that you have already studied, either at GCSE or AS Level, or one that you have recently read. Start by making a list of potential texts for transformation.

You can add to this list as you read over the summer holiday. Do not confine yourself to novels, but look for collections of short stories and poetry. The smaller scale of such literary works may be more feasible to work on, but you may also select an extract from a novel. If you see a play at the theatre or on television, try to find a copy of the original script.

Once you have a few ideas for texts, you will be ready to start on another piece of your own writing!

Commentaries

Activity 1

Some students assess extract 1 as the 'best', because they find it complex, difficult and dull! This is a worrying definition of 'good' writing and causes some students to attempt an over formal, dry style in their writing, regardless of the purpose, audience and genre.

Some students choose extract 2, because it is short, clear and simple. Being as clear and simple as possible is sometimes effective.

Some choose extract 4, because it appeals to their age group. This is clearly effective, if your target audience is students.

Perhaps some of you chose extract 3? It is also personal and colloquial, but would appeal more to older people.

The response you should have made is that it is impossible to answer the question, 'Which extract is the best?' You need to know more details, such as 'best for what situation?' Each of these extracts could be perfectly effective for a particular purpose, audience and genre. This module does not test writing skills 'in a vacuum'. If you produce a text without a clear sense of the context, you will not achieve a high mark. Therefore it is essential to be absolutely clear about the three factors of purpose, audience and genre. Extract 1 is taken from a specialist cookery book and gives the amount of detail that would appeal to cookery enthusiasts. Extract 2 summarises the information in a brief manner that would be suitable for a 'cut-out and keep' cookery card. Extract 3 presents the information in a more colloquial manner that might be suitable for a daytime cookery programme or a women's magazine. Extract 4 is aimed at a student audience and has the secondary purposes of entertaining and persuading.

Activity 2

There were probably many similarities in the points made. Most people worry that their spelling, punctuation or style of writing is not good enough. This makes them self-conscious about showing their writing to other people and dread the negative reaction that might follow. However, most people also remember times when they loved writing and the chance to express themselves. There is a lot of pleasure in working carefully and feeling proud of the final product. Conversation never gives us the chance to talk without interruption, to plan words carefully and go back and change parts that didn't quite work the first time.

Activity 3

In this exercise, people tend to portray the woman in one of two ways, as either a gangster's moll or a downtrodden wife. It is rare to see a strong young woman in hiking boots, or a power-dressed business woman.

There are clearly two main stories here suggested by the description of the man. Think back to the section on metonyms on page 30. In Britain there are certain cultural stereotypes around suits for example, but the reference to gold watch and rings moves the image away from straight businessman and the scar immediately signals violence, even though it could have been caused by a car accident. Your choice of items of clothing and appearance probably also signalled the woman as a type to your readers.

Activity 4

Writers' handbooks often mention the importance of *showing* rather than *telling*. In the first piece of writing, you did not *tell* the reader anything directly about the character, but your description may have revealed as much. Every day we have to guess at what people are like by observing them. It was probably not necessary for you, as the writer, to step in and explain in abstract terms, for example 'She was apprehensive, but disguised her fear by appearing confident.' Readers often prefer to make these judgements for themselves. Impressions made this way can be much more subtle than if the character is summed up in a short phrase.

Activity 5

These are the points made by one group of students.

Positive aspects. The tone is sympathetic, showing the feelings of a bullied child in the 1st-person quotations right at the beginning. It's quite an unusual way to start, so catches the attention of the reader.

The advice is given in a positive and reassuring tone, using capitals, underlining and exclamation marks for emphasis.

The sentence structure is simple and colloquial vocabulary is used, so this is appropriate for the audience. It finishes with catchy slogans that are positive.

Critical comments. The tone is rather sensational and patronising. Are the feelings mentioned exaggerated and predictable, particularly when highlighted in a bold list?

The colloquialism 'eggs on' is rather odd and not really part of a young person's speech.

The promises of help sound like sales patter in their overstatement, 'forever'. The soundbites at the end are too corny.

Too many exclamation marks and capital letters are used.

Who is this 'I' making the promises?

Martin has disappeared by the end and should be mentioned again with the problem resolved.

Activity 7

1   The spoken piece is a monologue rather than a conversation and has been planned, implicitly at least, to keep to the same topic throughout.

However, there are some features of interaction in the 'asides' – extra comments expressing the speaker's opinions to the friend, for example 'official name Cerberus in case you cared' and 'it's a lot of fun'. The friend is addressed directly as 'you' and the speaker refers to themselves as 'I': 'do you know what I mean' and 'let me think'.

It is spontaneous speech, so there are non-fluency features such as 'erm' and self-corrections: 'no go through to the map room sorry'. Noun phrases are repeated: 'get the shotgun always shoot your shotgun', rather than using the pronoun 'it' instead.

There is much use of co-ordination: 'well anyway get that *and* put that in the tiger statue thing *and* once you've killed the snake go through the garden *and* go to the guard house'. This quote also shows the use of conversational markers such as 'well anyway' and imprecise vocabulary such as 'tiger statue thing'.

2 The written version is much briefer and uses headings and numbered lists to make the progression of tips clear. Other markers such as 'first', 'next', 'then' emphasise the progression.

Each instruction is phrased as an imperative: 'hide', 'do not shoot'.

There is no reference to the writer, but the reader is occasionally addressed as 'you'. There are no personal, evaluative comments.

Activity 8

Extract 1 begins in a detached tone, simply giving information about the club: in the first two sentences, the team is referred to in the 3rd person 'their'. The 1st person pronoun 'we' occurs in the third sentence and seems an odd intrusion. This leaflet now seems to be written *by* the club, rather than about it, so it no longer sounds like unbiased information. This sense of an in-crowd continues with the use of 'we' and 'our' and the unexplained reference to a 'constructors championship' – whatever that is. The final paragraph adopts a jokey tone with subjective opinions and mysterious references to winches, noses and spades. The writer suddenly introduces the 1st person singular into the text: 'Let me assure you' and adds a chatty comment in brackets. Unfortunately the reader is not in on the joke. The final assertion suggests stress on the word 'do', where the written form would be the more neutral 'You get sent your money's worth.'

Extract 2 uses bold print too often to emphasise words that do not seem particularly important. Using bold, capitals and exclamation marks is the visual equivalent of shouting. Bullet points are useful to present a concise list, so it is strange to include chatty discourse markers here. It is very rare for there to be an 'I' in leaflets. They tend to be disembodied information rather than a personal statement. This writer is intruding into the text far too much with personal details and comments. It's surely not necessary to point out the picture to readers. The writer then changes to 'we', suggesting a cosy ramble arm-in-arm through the leaflet. The reader will probably be irritated / alienated by the egotistical tone.

Activity 9

The progression is clearly indicated by a variety of phrases introducing each topic: 'Good morning and welcome', 'Firstly', 'Other opportunities are also', 'Apart from clubs and societies', 'On a more serious note', 'Lastly', 'Well that's the end of my talk.'

In order to suggest some interaction between speaker and listener, the speaker refers to themselves in the 1st person: 'My name is', 'Trust me. I know.' The listeners are occasionally directly addressed in the 2nd person: 'you, the newly enrolled students', 'if you want to talk to someone'.

The tone is generally quite detached and formal (which you may feel is not effective for the audience) but there are some colloquial phrases, such as 'for all of you chess masters', and a few evaluative comments from the speaker, such as 'fantastic trips'.

Activity 11

The writer adopts the persona of a primary-school teacher, but includes stylistic features of a funeral speech. The purpose is to entertain by this amusing clash of styles.

There are many examples of the language of a funeral oration: 'to pay respect to someone close to us all, who we sadly lost'. This register often uses the rhetorical devices of triples and balanced phrases: 'a hamster I am proud to call my friend, the unique, the complex, the irreplaceable Floozy, who gave so much and asked for so little in return.'

There are also many examples of the register of a primary-school assembly: 'They seemed to find her toilet problem more interesting', 'Some, especially Harry Field and his disciples, thought that writing "Poozy Floozy" across the pet corner sign would make them look hard.'

The previous quote shows some mixing of registers in the term 'disciples'. However, the main incongruity comes from the clash of semantic fields – a hamster is a most unlikely subject for a funeral oration and the inclusion of 'hamster terms' in grand praise is hilarious: 'her own brand of furry magic' and 'Your beautiful face with your tickling whiskers'.

There may not be agreement on the parts that should be cut. Some humour arises from the shock value of mentioning taboos such as death and bodily functions and audience reactions vary from laughter to disapproval. You may feel that the 'toilet humour' is too crude and would cut the paragraph referring to her as 'a dollop on the floor'. The writer herself was aware that there was a risk in referring to a well-known speech and death, so included an 'apology'. You may want to cut any allusion to a real person. These issues are significant in writing a commentary on a humorous text that risks taste boundaries.

Activity 13

These are the comments made in note form by one student.

Balance. 'Back to school'; 'still snow on the ground'. Peaceful weather and normal occurrences don't suggest any drama happening.

Beginning. 'Tony wasn't ...' – past tense implies disaster. 'It's their fault' – blame suggests something happening that shouldn't have.

Problem. 'He felt like a man on the moon', 'He just had to stay there forever.'

Disharmony. Violence towards a teenager: 'They push you ... kick you ...'.

Inciting moment. Bullying. Not stated, so is left to vivid imagination.

End. Tragedy, running away, but suggestion of suicide.

Resolution. Isn't one; the resolution must be carried out by the audience in their everyday life, as it is an assembly story.

Perspective. Personal and pitiful.

Theme. Bullying, effect on the family.

Activity 15

Readers have to be interested if they are going to read on. Sometimes the story itself is exciting or interesting enough: car crashes, death of a celebrity, etc., but, more often than not, the journalist has to provide that first bit of interest themselves.

Humour is one way of capturing interest. In headings, puns are popular: 'putt it into perspective'.

Another way of getting someone's attention is by sounding excited yourself. Some writers have used very short sentences and exclamation marks. 'Part-time work!'

Some writers started the article with a short statement, leaping straight into the argument. This gives the reader a sense of business and speed. 'America was first. Britain is next.'

Overstatement is more arresting than a cautious claim: 'adults and children alike clutching at their light sabres and worshipping their Jedi figures'.

Addressing the reader directly, often with a question, is a way of demanding attention. The reader is encouraged to think about their answer and to read on to see what the writer says: 'have you ever wondered what all the fuss is about?' Of course, if the answer is 'No, I haven't' you may lose the reader at this point. It would be safer to ask, 'What is all the fuss about?' You can use the pronoun 'we' to include the reader, assuming that the writer and reader share the same point of view. The reader may switch off, if they don't: 'Not only are we tuning in to watch [soaps], but we're buying magazines, posters ...'. You could, instead, offer a personal slant and hope that the reader shares it: 'Even the sound of this makes my toes curl.'

Ambivalent or mysterious starts can interest the reader before they even know what the subject of the text is: 'I'm tired, my stomach is making water buffalo mating calls and I'm finding it hard to see.'

There are a couple of openings that don't provoke interest, for example writing the way someone would introduce a dull radio or TV programme: 'Welcome my friends to another heated debate on ...' or ' This week *Overrated* is looking at arguably the most ...'

It is not a good idea to be tentative in your opening. The feature article is not like a balanced essay, but a strong argument. The writers of openings 4 and 7 have included cautious disclaimers. If you take out the words and phrases in italics, the opening has more impact: 'Nightclubs have become *something of* an institution *in themselves*', '*It can be said that* Britain really has gone soap crazy.'

It is also not important to explain key terms, as you might in the introduction to an essay. Notice also how the writers of openings 1 and 4 have adopted a formal style, using passive forms of the verb. 'It cannot be forgotten though that part-time work is a necessity for many ...'. It is certainly not necessary to explain what nightclubs are: 'They *are found* in every town and city and are the most popular form of entertainment ...'.

If you are writing for a specific audience, you can refer to things, which help to identify the group and exclude other readers. Opening 9 would work well in a men's magazine, by deliberately mentioning drink, drugs and girls in the first paragraph.

Unless you are writing for an extremely selective magazine, you shouldn't put too much technical information or specialist jargon in an opening sentence, as this will just confuse and scare off the general reader. So, unless you think everybody knows what 'TSR and AD&D' stand for, don't use too much jargon.

Activity 17

Extract 1 addresses the reader directly as 'you' and refers to themself as 'I'. They adopt a speaking style, using brackets to suggest a thought that has just occurred to them.

Extract 2 uses a number of colloquial features effectively. The reader is addressed immediately with a minor interrogative, followed by the colloquial phrase 'me too'. The points are made from a personal angle, using the pronoun 'I', often including the audience with the plural 'we'. Questions are often used (though the lack of punctuation spoils the effect). Imperatives are used to round off the points in a dynamic way: 'Don't put us second best when we want to be first'. There are colloquial phrases, such as 'get a bit tedious'. There are conversational markers, such as 'now' and 'so', to start sentences and fillers, such as 'alright' and 'surely' within sentences.

Not all colloquial features are effective, however. A personal touch can be appealing, but too many references to the writer's own thought processes are dull. Extract 1 uses phrases like this often: 'I believe', 'in my opinion'.

We may use adverbs like 'really', 'probably' and 'surely' a lot when speaking, but written text tends to work better if these are taken out.

Both writers create a speaking voice with fillers to introduce statements, for example 'Then again', 'I mean, alright'. These might be too leisurely and are certainly a point to consider in re-drafting.

Extract 2 uses some long, loosely co-ordinated sentences, which are not punctuated clearly. This happens in the third sentence of the first paragraph, so the style lacks clarity and impact. Check whether long sentences can be followed easily, when reading from the page.

Activity 19

Extract 1 was written by a student in exam conditions; extract 2 was written by Julie Burchill for her regular column in the *Guardian Weekend* magazine. Both writers use similar emotional appeals and stylistic techniques, but perhaps the professional journalist's text seemed more 'polished'?

Extract 1 asks many questions of the audience, whereas Julie Burchill asks one. However, she addresses the audience directly with imperatives at the end of the article. These are also balanced phrases: 'Don't make that deadline; take the long way home.' Both writers offer their own opinions, though the writer of extract 1 refers to 'I' more often. Both adopt an aggressive tone, possibly complimenting the audience implicitly, by implying we are not like the others. Both mock and disparage the views of their opponents. The use of emotive words with negative connotations is obvious in both texts – one using the image of rats and the other using references to boring people and 'drones'. Both use exaggeration: 'countless', 'the world will end'. Julie Burchill uses opposites in balanced phrases: 'less–more' 'martyrs–egoists'. Her use of threes is repeated, so that it builds up to a climax. The writer of extract 1 repeats the phrases 'Millions of pounds' in three successive sentences, building up, or down, to the minor sentence: 'Build a dome.'

Activity 23

1 The tone of the opening is intended to be friendly and reassuring, but the use of exclamation marks after the first two sentences may not be calming. Similar helpful comments are made at the end, but perhaps the exclamation marks should be cut.

   The headings are often single words, but there are two longer ones. It might be better to keep the style consistent.

2 The numbered list consistently uses imperatives, so the final item 7 seems out of place and actually repeats previous advice. The use of three phrases like a slogan could be effective and memorable. It would be better to take out the exclamation marks from other advice, particularly after 'Stay calm'.

   The list with bullet points does not have the necessary consistency. Most points are imperatives, but there are some exceptions. The first point should be the introductory sentence; the third point is part of the second. It might be better to avoid the detailed examples about breakfast and appearance, so that the points could be a brief summary.

Activity 26

Discourse. Writer–reader relationship assumes shared interests and knowledge. Modern mixture of colloquial and formal styles.

Overall structure. A 'hook' beginning and a standard assessment at the end, in keeping with the genre.

Grammar. Variety of sentence structures, mainly complex, but simple for contrast.

Vocabulary. Technical jargon is mixed with slang and everyday terms, so the text doesn't seem too 'geeky' and obsessive. High-level vocabulary shows authority.

Graphology. Not mentioned.

Content. Provides details and opinions.

Glossary

Abstract: describing the quality of a thing apart from the thing itself

Adjective: a word added to a noun to qualify it, e.g. large

Adverb: a word added to a verb, adjective, or other adverb to modify its meaning, e.g. fast

Alliteration: a resemblance of sound (either vowels or consonants) between two syllables in nearby words

Archaic, archaism: terms referring to language features that are no longer in use

Assonance: a repetition within successive words of similar vowel sounds

Audience: the person or people at whom material is directed

Channel: the mode by which a communication is transmitted, e.g. the channel for speech is sounds

Collocation: this describes words that tend to occur in a particular context with others

Colloquial: used in common expressions, informal use of language

Conjunction: a word that connects sentences, clauses and words, e.g. and

Connotation: not so much the surface meaning of the word, as what it implies or suggests, i.e. home = 'warmth'

Consonance: a recurrence of similar-sounding consonants

Consonant: a speech sound other than a vowel

Context: the purpose and audience of a text, including whether it is written or spoken and its social and historical setting

Convergence: a tendency to behave like other people with whom a person has contact

Dated, old-fashioned: no longer in common usage

Denotation: the surface meaning of the word

Determiner: a limiting adjective or modifying word, e.g. any, my

Diachronic variation: variation in the language that occurs over time

Dialogue: a spoken interaction involving more than one person

Discourse markers: words and phrases that signal the structure and organisation of the text

Divergence: a tendency to behave differently from people with whom a person has no contact

Ellipsis: an abbreviation in which a word or words are left out and implied

External narration: where teller is not present as a character in the story

Figurative language: similes, metaphors, metonyms, symbols and other non-literal uses of language

Foregrounding: bringing something to your attention, rather than keeping it out of the way (**deviation**: breaking the usual pattern) (**parallelism**: creating patterns by repetition)

Formal: in proper, perhaps ceremonious, form

Generic term: an expression that refers to the whole group

Genre: a recognisable form or type of text that is governed by the way the particular texts are written for particular purposes

Geographical dialect: evidence in the words or sound of the language of the speaker's regional origin

Grammar: the science of language

Graphological: to do with the appearance of the written word, conventions such as capital letters, underlining, italics, exclamation marks

Graphology: those features which contribute to the visual appearance of a text on the page

Grice's maxims – co-operative principle: the philosopher, Paul Grice, suggested that conversation will work well if participants stick to four general principles: Quantity (you should provide neither too much nor too little); Relevance (you should keep your comments relevant); Quality (do not say what you believe to be false); Manner (do not make your contribution ambiguous or difficult to understand)

Idiolect: an individual's distinctive style of language

Internal narration: where the teller is one of the characters in the story

Jargon: the words used by a particular group or profession

Labov's framework: a six-part structure in oral narratives identified by William Labov: (1) abstract; (2) orientation; (3) complicating action; (4) evaluation; (5) result or resolution; (6) coda

Lexis: the collective term for the vocabulary of a language

Metaphor: a figure of speech in which something is spoken of as being something that it resembles (**extended metaphor**: other words related to the original metaphor)

Metonym: an image in which part of something stands for the whole

Monologue: a composition intended to be spoken by one person

Morphology: the way that words are formed from smaller units of meaning – morphemes, e.g. the word un-reli-able is formed from three morphemes: the **prefix** (un-) adds a negative sense to the **base** (rely) and the **suffix** (-able) includes the concept of ability

Narrative: an orderly account of a series of events which has three elements: a teller, a tale and a tellee

Narrative voice: the perspective from which the story is related (**1st person**: where narration is coming from the character to whom the event is occurring) (**3rd person**: where the narration comes from an outsider, or one of the other characters involved in the situation) (**omniscient narrator**: where the narrator, who is not present as a character in the story, knows the character well enough to be able to make judgements and comments) (**flawed narrator**: where the character relating the story is presented as being unreliable)

Neologism: a new word or phrase (**borrowing**: taken from another language) (**compounding**: joining two words together) (**acronym**: based on or formed from the initial letters or syllables of other words) (**blending**: merging two or more words together) (**clipping**: abbreviating a word)

Non-finite verb: there are three non-finite verb forms: 'to' + verb (*to err* is human); verb + '-ing' (*peering* through the letterbox, she called his name); verb + '-ed' (*exhausted* by the journey, he slept soundly)

Noun: a word used as a name, usually preceded by a determiner

Noun phrase: group of words used as one noun

Onomatopoeia: a word the sound of which seems to resemble the thing that it refers to

Parenthesis: a word or passage inserted into a sentence that is grammatically complete without it

Perspective: the position and distance from which events are viewed (**1st person**: the character to whom the event is occurring) (**3rd person**: an outsider, or one of the other characters involved in the situation)

Phonology: the study of those aspects of language connected to its sound

Phrase: a group of words expressing an idea

Plot: a plan or design

Point of view, perspective: the position and distance from which events are viewed

Polysyllabic: a word with many or more than three syllables

Preposition: word most commonly occuring before a noun, indicating position in time or space, e.g. under the table; on Saturday evening

Pronoun: a word used instead of a noun, e.g. she (**1st person**: I, we, one) (**2nd person**: you) (**3rd person**: he, she, it, they)

Proper noun: one type of noun referring to names of people, products, places, institutions, and that is written with a capital letter

Purpose: the function of the text, what it is trying to do

Register: the (appropriate) style of language for a situation, social or occupational group (**formal**: a proper style appropriate for example to a ceremonial occasion) (**informal**: a style appropriate for example to a chat with friends)

Representation of speech: the way in which speech or thought is related (**narrator summary of speech**: where the narrator sums the speech up) (**direct speech**: where the speech is recorded inside speech marks, with some indication of who was speaking) (**free direct speech**: where the words spoken are put simply on separate lines, rather as in a drama script) (**indirect speech**: where the narrator records the speech, there are some grammatical changes to the form of the words) (**free indirect speech**: where the words are reported in the past tense without an introductory reporting clause like 'she said')

Rhyme: a correspondence in sound between words (**half-rhyme**: where the sound is the same but for one difference)

Semantic field: a grouping of words with related or similar meanings

Semantics: the study of words and their meanings: the dictionary definition and all the associated meanings

Sentence: a set of words complete as an expression of thought and conveying an idea

Sentence structure: the way a sentence is put together (**simple**: a sentence with only one verb group) (**compound**: sentences or clauses linked simply by 'and' or 'but') (**complex**: where there are subordinate clauses bound together by connectives such as 'which', 'that, 'if', etc., or verbs endings in '-ing' or '-ed' (**minor**: a fragment of a sentence) (**declarative**: the most common type of sentence, a statement) (**imperative**: a command) (**interrogative**: a question)

Simile: a figure of speech that makes an explicit comparison between two things

Social dialect: features in the words or sound of the language that are common to a social group (**Standard English (SE)**: the dialect previously spoken in areas around London, Oxford and Cambridge, accepted as the model for educated written usage in the UK) (**non-standard**: dialect that doesn't conform to any standards) (**Received Pronunciation (RP)**: the standard form of pronunciation) (**Estuary English**: a modified version of RP that may drop 'aitches' and use glottal stops instead of the plosive consonant 't', e.g. I haven(–) go(–) a lo(–)'

Speech: something that is spoken

Story: a narrative of incidents in their sequence

Subordinating conjunction: a connecting word that introduces a new clause, e.g that

Symbol: an image that is used to represent something else

Synchronic variation: variation in the language that occurs at any one point in time

Synonym: a word that has the same meaning as another word

Temporal dialect: features in a spoken language that are distinctive in a time in history

Tense: the form of a verb that indicates the time of an action (**present tense**: something happening now) (**past tense**: something that did, or used to, happen)

Transcript: a written representation of words as they are actually spoken (**pauses**: a temporary stop) (**repetition**: something said several times) (**false start**: where the speaker begins, pauses, and then starts again in a completely different direction) (**self-correction**: where the speaker starts speaking and then has to rephrase the sentence)

Verb: a part of speech that indicates an action

Vowel: a speech sound (a, e, i, o, u)

Word class: the type of word: noun, verb, adjective, adverb, pronoun, preposition, determiner or conjunction

Writing: a (literary or non-literary) production that has been written down

Further reading

English Language and Literature: an Integrated Approach Ron Norman (Nelson Thornes, 1998)

Working with Texts Ronald Carter, Angela Goddard, Danuta Reah, Keith Sanger, Maggie Bowring (Routledge, 1997; 2nd ed, 2001)

Language and Gender Angela Goddard, Lindsay Mean Patterson (Routledge, 2000)

Living Language and Literature George Keith, John Shuttleworth (Hodder and Stoughton, 2000)

Language Change R. L. Trask (Routledge, 1994)

Ways of Reading Martin Montgomery, Alan Durant, Sara Mills, Nigel Fabb, Tom Furniss (Routledge, 2nd ed 2000)

The Literature Workbook Clara Calvo, Jean Jacques Weber (Routledge, 1998)